D0085220

DATE DUE

MR 12 '01			
AP 22 '0?			
MR 01 '04			
AP 21 '06			
NO 16 '06			
NOV 3 0 2006			
	WITHDRAWN		

Demco, Inc. 38-293

TERRY McMILLAN

A Critical Companion

Paulette Richards

WITHDRAWN

CRITICAL COMPANIONS TO POPULAR CONTEMPORARY WRITERS
Kathleen Gregory Klein, Series Editor

813
M16721

Greenwood Press
Westport, Connecticut • **London**

LIBRARY
MILWAUKEE AREA TECHNICAL COLLEGE
Milwaukee Campus

Library of Congress Cataloging-in-Publication Data

Richards, Paulette.
    Terry McMillan : a critical companion / Paulette Richards.
      p. cm.—(Critical companions to popular contemporary
writers, ISSN 1082–4979)
    Includes bibliographical references (p.) and index.
    ISBN 0–313–30504–8 (alk. paper)
    1. McMillan, Terry—Criticism and interpretation. 2. Women and
literature—United States—History—20th century. 3. Afro-Americans
in literature. I. Title. II. Series.
PS3563.C3868Z87   1999
813'.54—dc21   99–27177

British Library Cataloguing in Publication Data is available.

Copyright © 1999 by Paulette Richards

All rights reserved. No portion of this book may be
reproduced, by any process or technique, without
the express written consent of the publisher.

Library of Congress Catalog Card Number: 99–27177
ISBN: 0–313–30504–8
ISSN: 1082–4979

First published in 1999

Greenwood Press, 88 Post Road West, Westport, CT 06881
An imprint of Greenwood Publishing Group, Inc.
www.greenwood.com

Printed in the United States of America

The paper used in this book complies with the
Permanent Paper Standard issued by the National
Information Standards Organization (Z39.48–1984).

10 9 8 7 6 5 4 3 2 1

ILLINOIS
VALLEY AREA TECHNICAL COLLEGE
Milwaukee Campus

To Deborah E. McDowell who is an unwavering beacon.

ADVISORY BOARD

Mary Catherine Byrd, English Teacher, East Montgomery High School, Biscoe, North Carolina

Dr. Dana McDougald, Library Media Specialist, Cedar Shoals High School, Athens, Georgia

Patricia Naismith, Library Media Specialist, Springfield High School, Springfield, Pennsylvania

Italia Negroni, Head, Library Media Technology Department, Stamford High School, Stamford, Conneticut

Rudy Rocamontes, Jr., English Teacher, Southwest High School, San Antonio, Texas

Alice F. Stern, Young Adults Librarian, Boston Public Library, Boston, Massachusetts

Marcia Welsh, Assistant Director, Guilford Free Library, Guilford, Connecticut

Contents

Series Foreword

The authors who appear in the series Critical Companions to Popular Contemporary Writers are all best-selling writers. They do not simply have one successful novel, but a string of them. Fans, critics, and specialist readers eagerly anticipate their next book. For some, high cash advances and breakthrough sales figures are automatic; movie deals often follow. Some writers become household names, recognized by almost everyone.

But, their novels are read one by one. Each reader chooses to start and, more importantly, to finish a book because of what she or he finds there. The real test of a novel is in the satisfaction its readers experience. This series acknowledges the extraordinary involvement of readers and writers in creating a best-seller.

The authors included in this series were chosen by an Advisory Board composed of high school English teachers and high school and public librarians. They ranked a list of best-selling writers according to their popularity among different groups of readers. For the first series, writers in the top-ranked group who had received no book-length, academic, literary analysis (or none in at least the past ten years) were chosen. Because of this selection method, Critical Companions to Popular Contemporary Writers meets a need that is being addressed nowhere else. The success of these volumes as reported by reviewers, librarians, and teachers led to an expansion of the series mandate to include some writers with wide critical attention—Toni Morrison, John Irving, and Maya Angelou, for example—to extend the usefulness of the series.

The volumes in the series are written by scholars with particular expertise in analyzing popular fiction. These specialists add an academic focus to the popular success that these writers already enjoy.

The series is designed to appeal to a wide range of readers. The general reading public will find explanations for the appeal of these well-known writers. Fans will find biographical and fictional questions answered. Students will find literary analysis, discussions of fictional genres, carefully organized introductions to new ways of reading the novels, and bibliographies for additional research. Whether browsing through the book for pleasure or using it for an assignment, readers will find that the most recent novels of the authors are included.

Each volume begins with a biographical chapter drawing on published information, autobiographies or memoirs, prior interviews, and, in some cases, interviews given especially for this series. A chapter on literary history and genres describes how the author's work fits into a larger literary context. The following chapters analyze the writer's most important, most popular, and most recent novels in detail. Each chapter focuses on one or more novels. This approach, suggested by the Advisory Board as the most useful to student research, allows for an in-depth analysis of the writer's fiction. Close and careful readings with numerous examples show readers exactly how the novels work. These chapters are organized around three central elements: plot development (how the story line moves forward), character development (what the reader knows of the important figures), and theme (the significant ideas of the novel). Chapters may also include sections on generic conventions (how the novel is similar, or different from others in its same category of science fiction, fantasy, thriller, etc.), narrative point of view (who tells the story and how), symbols and literary language, and historical or social context. Each chapter ends with an "alternative reading" of the novel. The volume concludes with a primary and secondary bibliography, including reviews.

The alternative readings are a unique feature of this series. By demonstrating a particular way of reading each novel, they provide a clear example of how a specific perspective can reveal important aspects of the book. In the alternative reading sections, one contemporary literary theory—way of reading, such as feminist criticism, Marxism, new historicism, deconstruction, or Jungian psychological critique—is defined in brief, easily comprehensible language. That definition is then applied to the novel to highlight specific features that might go unnoticed or be understood differently in a more general reading. Each volume defines two or three specific theories, making them part of the reader's understanding of how diverse meanings may be constructed from a single novel.

Taken collectively, the volumes in the Critical Companions to Popular Contemporary Writers series provide a wide-ranging investigation of the complexities of current best-selling fiction. By treating these novels seriously as both literary works and publishing successes, the series demonstrates the potential of popular literature in contemporary culture.

Kathleen Gregory Klein
Southern Connecticut State University

Acknowledgments

Thanks first and foremost to Gina and Andrew Macdonald who extended themselves above and beyond the call of duty in showing me the ropes. I thank Kevin Meehan for graciously lending an ear and for coaching me in the finer points of socialist realism. Numerous conversations with Harriet Margolis sharpened my knowledge of popular romance forms and I am especially grateful for her patience with my theories about conjure. Brenda Square and Rebecca Hankins at the Amistad Research Center helped me track down many periodicals. Their enthusiasm for this project has sustained my efforts. As always my brother Charles Richards supported me with abundant love and encouragement. Finally thanks to Peter, Caridad, and Barbara for guiding me through this journey.

The Life of Terry McMillan

Terry McMillan's ability to draw on her own life experiences and evoke her own emotional truth in her novels is one important element of her tremendous popular appeal. McMillan sees her novels as a record of her own spiritual growth; consequently, her formal structure changes with each work. Indeed, while the literary establishment has dismissed Terry McMillan as a popular fiction writer, her continual manipulation of popular women's fiction genre conventions to suit her own artistic ends is a measure of her talent and skill. Although McMillan garnered several prestigious awards early in her career, her commercial success has made academic critics reluctant to recognize her as a serious writer. Yet McMillan has made important contributions as a teacher, scholar, and mentor to younger writers in addition to inspiring a whole new school of urban black fiction. The question of McMillan's ultimate critical reception remains open. Still, her life and works offer an eloquent testimonial on human individuals' capacity to imagine and create fulfilling lives for themselves.

EARLY YEARS

Terry Y. McMillan was born October 18, 1951, in Port Huron, Michigan, the oldest of five children. Her father, Edward Lewis McMillan, died of complications related to diabetes when Terry was sixteen. Her mother, Madeline Washington Tillman, was the sustaining force in her life. Despite her mother's lack of education, McMillan was deeply impressed by her innate intelligence: "For an uneducated woman, she's probably one of the smartest women I'll ever meet in my life. She taught me how to think, that's what she did. And to let people know what you think. And if you don't have an opinion about something, get one, because you'll need it" (quoted in Hershenson). In addition to her intelligence and her determination to teach her children to cope aggressively with life, Madeline was also very strong willed. She did not passively accept the blows life dealt her. McMillan remembers that when he was drunk, her father would try to beat her mother, but Madeline always fought back. McMillan recalls that sometimes she won.

When McMillan was thirteen, her parents divorced. After this separation, Madeline exerted an even more powerful influence on her children. She worked in a variety of jobs from domestic work to auto assembly lines and even did a stint in a pickle factory in order to support her children. At times, she also applied for welfare to supplement her income. Nevertheless, McMillan says, "There were a couple of winter nights I remember my teeth chattering. . . . But I don't remember ever feeling poor. I hate that word. We never went hungry" (quoted in Leland).

Madeline instilled a strong sense of responsibility in her children early in their lives. While she was away at work, she expected them to keep the house neat and stay out of trouble. The McMillan children also did odd jobs so that they could contribute to the household budget. Terry's sister Rosalyn was raking leaves to earn money by the time she was eight years old. She remembers big sister Terry as a hardworking "little mother" who cooked, cleaned, fixed hair, and took care of the other children from an early age (Hubbard and Rowlands 107). When she was sixteen, Terry landed her first paying job. She shelved books in the St. Clair Country Library for $1.25 an hour.

The only book in the McMillan household during Terry's childhood was the Bible. The library job opened up the world of books for her. McMillan specifically remembers identifying with a biography of Louisa May Alcott because Alcott had to help support her family when she was very young (Smith 50). She also enjoyed the novels of the Brontë sisters. Thus, she gained an early grounding in the traditions of women's fiction. Discovering the works of James Baldwin was an important revelation to her since nothing in her experience up to that point had indicated that black people could write and publish books. At the time, she had no ambition to write herself. Indeed, she recalls that she was too afraid to read his book, adding, "I couldn't imagine that he'd have anything better or different to say than Thomas Mann, Henry Thoreau, Ralph Waldo Emerson" (quoted in Thompson 774). Nevertheless, the job in the library allowed her to dream of a life very different from the one she knew. She would often sit in the stacks poring through travel books and fantasizing about visiting far-flung places. These fantasies helped bolster her determination to get out of Port Huron when she grew up.

EDUCATION

The dream of a better life gave the teenaged McMillan the discipline and ambition to make something of herself even though she did not yet know what that something would be. While her friends were experimenting with sex, she resisted. She was determined to finish high school to escape the projects, and to avoid raising a string of babies for which she would refuse government assurance. Once she had completed high school, McMillan left Port Huron for Los Angeles with the $300 she had saved working as a keypunch operator. For the first time, she was on her own. But she remained true to her goals. By day she worked as a typist for an insurance company, but at night she took classes at Los Angeles City College.

One class that profoundly influenced her was a course in African American literature. In this class, she finally read with deep appreciation the works of James Baldwin. Additionally, she cites Langston Hughes as one of the writers on the syllabus who particularly impressed her. Indeed, in her own writing, McMillan has carried on Hughes's efforts to capture the rhythms of black vernacular speech in print. A vocabulary class in which she learned five hundred new words in one semester helped McMillan unlock the power of language. A poem she wrote to express her heartbreak over the end of a relationship made her realize what a satisfying tool writing could be for expressing her feelings.

McMillan did so well at City College that she was able to transfer to the University of California at Berkeley to complete her degree. It was there that her interest in writing began to manifest itself. She majored in journalism and frequently contributed articles to the *Daily Californian* and *Black Thoughts*, two student newspapers. She also enrolled in a creative writing workshop conducted by Ishmael Reed, a noted African American

novelist and poet. McMillan's ear for dialogue made a strong impression
on Reed, but he was even more impressed by her drive: "Talent is very
common. But fewer people have the will, the energy and the drive to
get over. Terry had that" (quoted in Spratling).

COMMITMENT TO WRITING

In 1979, after finishing her bachelor of science degree at Berkeley, Mc-
Millan traveled across the country to pursue a master's degree in the
Fine Arts in Film Program at Columbia University in New York City.
Like her decision to major in journalism as an undergraduate, this decision to earn a graduate degree in film studies confirms McMillan's
maturing sense of purpose and her growing desire to communicate with
a mass audience. Unfortunately, film school did not fulfill her expectations. She felt that she and an African student, the only blacks in the
class, were treated unfairly (Wilkerson 52). She left the program twenty-
six credits short of acquiring her master's but spent several more years
in New York supporting herself by doing word processing. In this in-
terim, McMillan began to hone her skills as a writer. She joined the Harlem Writers Guild, received several grants and awards, and finally began
to draft her first novel, *Mama*.

McMillan faced many obstacles while working on this project. Her
romance with Leonard Welch had produced a son, Solomon. Although
McMillan had been involved with Welch for three years, she made the
difficult decision to leave him nine months after their son was born.
Suddenly McMillan found herself an aspiring writer and single mother
who had to work full-time. The discipline she learned in her early years
when she took care of her younger siblings served her well. She rose at
5:00 A.M. every morning and spent two hours working on her novel.
Then, she would pack up her small son and drop him off at day care on
the way to work. McMillan typed and printed her drafts at work during
her lunch hour. Fortunately, her coworkers and supervisors were supportive of her efforts.

Once the manuscript was completed, McMillan succeeded in selling it
to Houghton Mifflin, but the publisher was not willing to commit money
to advertise it or schedule a promotional tour. Conventional wisdom at
the time held that African Americans did not buy books. McMillan's
publisher believed her potential audience was so small that future sales
of book could not justify an advertising budget. McMillan, however,

knew that there was a large audience of black readers, and she believed that her novel, *Mama*, could reach that audience. She resolved to prove conventional wisdom wrong and set out to promote the book herself.

Terry McMillan sent out over three thousand letters to colleges, bookstores, and professional organizations describing her book and offering to give free public readings. As the responses came in, she scheduled her own book tour and perfected a reading style that drew on the familiar forms of the African American performance aesthetic. Her readings have been described as "camp meetings," alluding to the fact that McMillan's reading style echoes the techniques of African American preachers. Meanwhile, the word she brought to audiences made up predominantly of African American women was as cathartic as a good church service. McMillan made a very personal connection with the women who bought autographed copies of her book. They became a devoted core audience who spread the word about McMillan to their friends, family members, and book discussion groups. The thirty-nine readings McMillan gave to promote her first novel helped it sell through its first printing before it was released. *Mama* went into its third printing just six months after its initial release in 1987, and Terry McMillan was on her way.

WORKS

To date, Terry McMillan has published four novels, a number of uncollected short stories, and an edited volume of short stories by other African American authors. In addition, she has collaborated on the screenplays that translated *Waiting to Exhale* and *How Stella Got Her Groove Back* into movies. Commenting on the autobiographical elements that frequently appear in her fiction, McMillan has said that she views her novels as a chronicle of her own growth, and, indeed, each marks stages and changes in her life (Fitchner).

Mama (1987)

Mama depicts a strong-willed, working-class mother much like McMillan's own. The story is set in Point Haven, Michigan, during the 1960s and 1970s, an analogue of Port Huron, where McMillan spent her formative years. Like the McMillan family, the fictional Peacock brood consists of four girls and one boy. Freda, like her creator, Terry, is the oldest and often plays the "little mother" role, just as Terry did in her family. McMillan also has Freda share her dream of becoming rich and famous so that she can provide for her mother. McMillan more than realized this dream: in the last weeks before Madeline died, her devoted daughter had bought her a new house, a new Lexus, and a mouthful of teeth. The fictional Freda does not attain the same degree of material success, but she follows McMillan's route out of the ghetto. Freda escapes Michigan by moving to California after graduating from high school, just as her creator did. Also like her creator, Freda begins her higher education at the local community college but soon moves on, attending Stanford, the wealthier, aristocratic parallel to McMillan's Berkeley. Freda, like McMillan, majors in journalism and moves to New York City to pursue a master's degree—only Freda chooses to study journalism at New York University instead of film at Columbia. However, Freda also experiences the same disillusionment with graduate school that McMillan felt.

McMillan's ability to draw on and honestly translate her personal experience into her fiction is part of what makes her novels so emotionally compelling for her readers. Thus, her realistic depiction of Freda's struggle with alcohol addiction and recreational drug use is informed by personal experience. McMillan, however, is quick to point out that she gave up these self-destructive habits in the early 1980s, and she asserts that none of her present success would have been possible if she had continued these negative patterns.

Disappearing Acts (1989)

Whereas *Mama* grows out of gritty personal experience, *Disappearing Acts* provides more of a symbolic "portrait of the artist as a young woman." McMillan names her heroine after the great literary foremother of all African American women writers, Zora Neale Hurston. McMillan makes her Zora an aspiring singer rather than a writer. Yet, over the course of the novel, Zora evolves from performing songs to writing them. In this way, McMillan symbolizes her own debt to African American oral performance traditions. Further, Zora's desire to touch a mass audience and her vision of the function of art closely echo McMillan's own aesthetic practice.

The blues romance that McMillan portrays in the novel is also a composite of her own romantic experiences. The fictional hero of the story, Franklin, reports that he had dated a woman named Theresa who hated it if you called her Terri. Accordingly, McMillan suggests her intimate knowledge of this "fictional" man. In fact, seeing himself in McMillan's portrait of Franklin, her former live-in lover, Leonard Welch, filed a $4.75 million lawsuit against her and her publisher claiming defamation of character. He argued that there were too many parallels that would lead others to recognize Franklin as a portrait of himself—and an unflattering one at that. For example, Welch, like the fictional Franklin, was a carpenter. And just as he is the father of McMillan's son, Solomon, Franklin is the father of Zora's son, Jeremiah.

McMillan and many other writers worried that a ruling in favor of Welch would restrict their creative processes since, to varying degrees, most artists draw on real-life experience. The *Wall Street Journal* reported that the judge in the case did find parallels between the fictional character and the real man. He noted that they "share the same occupation and educational background and even like the same breakfast cereal." However, the judge stated that "the man in the novel is a lazy, emotionally disturbed alcoholic who uses drugs and sometimes beats his girlfriend" and declared that "Leonard Welch is none of these things" (quoted in Malinowski 423). Consequently, the New York Supreme Court ruled against Welch and dismissed his appeal in April 1991.

Waiting to Exhale (1992)

After this experience, McMillan chose to portray a supportive community of women in her next novel. All of McMillan's novels have featured strong bonds between women. Mildred Peacock of *Mama* raises four daughters. Zora from *Disappearing Acts* meets regularly with a group of three close women friends who offer her support and sisterly advice. In *Waiting to Exhale*, McMillan weaves the story around four "sistah friends" whom she endows with the foibles and experiences she has observed in herself and other black women of her acquaintance. The setting of the novel also reflects McMillan's own career move to Phoenix. In 1988, she accepted a position teaching creative writing at the University of Arizona. Savannah Jackson, the lead character in *Waiting to Exhale*, also moves to Phoenix in search of professional opportunities and eligible men. In Arizona, Savannah reconnects with her old college roommate, Bernadine Harris, and two friends Bernadine has made—Gloria Johnson, who runs the local beauty salon, and Robin Stokes, who is a regular patron and fellow member of Black Women on the Move, a community organization for professional black women.

McMillan says that the idea for the novel grew out of a telephone conversation she had with a woman friend about their mutual frustration with the dating scene. Professionally successful and attractive but left wondering why she was still alone, McMillan realized that many of her female friends were in the same plight. She therefore incorporated her friends' experiences as well as her own into her novel about successful professional women's distressing and failed search for love.

Never did she imagine that the story would touch such a responsive chord with so many women readers. She acknowledges that part of her success is due to the fact that she expressed something millions of women were feeling. McMillan also stresses that she did not intend the novel as an exercise in "male bashing." She points out that she did include some positive male characters but also refuses to apologize for the negative ones.

McMillan's original talent and determination enabled her to connect with a responsive audience of black female fans with her first two novels. *Waiting to Exhale* marked the point at which her work began to cross over and reach readers from all ethnic backgrounds. When the book became the second novel by a black woman writer to be adapted as a feature-length Hollywood film (Alice Walker's *The Color Purple* was the first), McMillan passed another milestone. Her message and characters touched the hearts of women nationwide.

Even more significant, however, was the fact that McMillan's success as a best-selling writer enabled her to negotiate a contract with Twentieth Century Fox that provided her with an unprecedented degree of artistic control over the project. On the recommendation of her friend, novelist Amy Tan, she chose Ron Bass to collaborate with her on the screenplay. Bass had adapted Tan's novel *The Joy Luck Club* into one of the few Hollywood films of the decade featuring the Asian American experience. McMillan took full advantage of her opportunity to portray positive African American characters on the big screen. She retained the title of executive producer and had the right of approval in selecting the director and cast (Gregory). Along with Forest Whitaker, her handpicked director, McMillan was instrumental in ensuring that many of the technical and managerial positions behind the scenes were filled with African Americans. This intervention allowed many minority film professionals to gain experience and/or union credentials. Often the Hollywood "old boy network" works to exclude people of color from access to such opportunities. McMillan used her clout to empower her own community.

The film was a box-office success, costing about $37 million to produce and grossing over $70 million. The soundtrack, featuring Whitney Houston, sold briskly. Yet this soundtrack, along with the film's actors was snubbed by the Motion Picture Academy when award time rolled around. The film did not receive any Oscar nominations. Still, for black women all around the country, attending the film during the 1995 Christmas season was a major social event. The birthday party scene also sparked a vogue for "*Waiting to Exhale* parties," where groups of women celebrated their lives and their friendships with one another.

How Stella Got Her Groove Back (1996)

In her first three novels, McMillan had depicted a middle-class African American experience of which the mainstream U.S. media had largely been unaware until the *Waiting to Exhale* phenomenon burst onto the scene. This same phenomenon catapulted the author to a level of wealth and power that most of her readers could experience only when fantasizing about "lifestyles of the rich and famous." When her fourth novel, *How Stella Got Her Groove Back*, was published, the popular press made much of McMillan's opulent new home in suburban Danville, California, an affluent suburb east of San Francisco. Eager readers gobbled up details about her clothes, jewelry, cars, and home décor with the same interest usually inspired by pop singers, sports heroes, and movie stars. McMillan herself catered to this appetite by shifting from her earlier realism to romantic fantasy in *Stella*. She made her heroine a financial analyst who had been able, through hard work and smart investments, to acquire the kind of material ease McMillan herself enjoyed. Stella's taste in interior design is very much like McMillan's. The purple leather tiles that grace both McMillan's real-life office and her fictional counterpart's office have sparked a lot of reader interest. Indeed, she gratified readers' fantasies of conspicuous consumption by sending Stella on frequent trips to Home Depot and the local mall and cataloguing her purchases in the pages of the novel. At the same time, Stella, like the author herself, begins her narrative struggling to get "back in the groove" after experiencing a number of personal tragedies.

By the time *Waiting to Exhale* was published, McMillan no longer had to schedule her own book tours. Her publisher, Viking Press, sent her on a six-week tour of twenty cities, beginning with a breakfast speech at the American Booksellers Association in Anaheim and closing with a reading at Central Park's SummerStage festival (Smith 50). In fact, during her *Stella* tour she became involved in an acrimonious exchange with the owner of an African American bookstore in St. Louis who charged that publishers and the national book chains were deliberately not scheduling black writers for appearances at black-owned bookstores ("Planned Protest Halts Book Signing").

Besides vulnerability to these kinds of attacks, the price of success also meant that McMillan had to spend far more time away from her family than she would have liked. While in London on a European sweep promoting *Waiting to Exhale*, she learned that her mother had suffered a fatal asthma attack. McMillan was still reeling from this loss when her good friend Doris Jean Austin died of liver cancer a year to the day after her mother's death. Bereft of her two closest confidantes, McMillan felt cast adrift. Although she had drafted over one hundred pages of a new novel entitled *A Day Late and a Dollar Short*, McMillan was at the time unable to complete the manuscript. The story line featured a strong mother figure much like her own, and her recent loss made it too painful to continue working on the book. McMillan had also not been able to resolve the frustration associated with her problems in finding a life partner, a frustration that she had expressed eloquently in *Waiting to Exhale*.

All of these factors combined left McMillan in an artistic and psychological rut. She could not write. She felt emotionally numb. Finally, she decided to take a vacation in a Jamaican resort. McMillan has described the epiphany she experienced in numerous interviews: "The sun. The breeze. The weather. The sand. I enjoyed it all. I felt my mother's spirit close by, and she told me to take happiness in the form in which it comes" (quoted in " 'Stella' in South Africa" 116). Perhaps the most important factor in her regeneration, however, was the love she found with Johnathan Plummer, a Jamaican man in his twenties. Once again, McMillan used her own life as a pattern for her art, describing in steamy detail forty-two-year-old Stella's romance with a twenty-one-year-old Jamaican man.

While promoting *How Stella Got Her Groove Back*, McMillan gave interviews and appeared on television with her son and new live-in lover. The older woman/younger man romance she enjoyed in her personal life and described in her fiction captured readers' interest. Still, while McMillan admits that *Stella* is "the most autobiographical thing I've written in a long time," she cautions that she is smart enough not to put her personal business in a book. Those who think they are reading a factual account of her relationship with Johnathan are fooling themselves, she warns. She has pointed out on several occasions that Winston Shakespeare, the hero of *Stella*, is a gourmet cook, while Johnathan cannot cook at all. She also differentiates between the two by saying that "Johnathan is not a hunk." The most significant difference between art and real life remains McMillan's prognosis for the relationship. Stella marries Winston and lives happily ever after. McMillan has not married Johnathan and consistently comments that the relationship works for now while acknowledging that it may not last. McMillan's attitude about her phenomenal success is similar. She recognizes that tomorrow the limelight could easily shift to someone else. Yet the future reception of her work is an intriguing question.

CRITICAL RECEPTION

Awards

Terry McMillan's exceptional talent and determination have won her fame, fortune, and fulfilling love. What she feels she has not received to date is respect for her artistry. Yet, before her phenomenal commercial success, McMillan had won several fellowships and awards recognizing her as a talented young writer. She received a Doubleday/Columbia University Literary Fellowship during her tenure in the master's program. She has been a three-time fellow at the Yaddo Artist Colony and has also attended the MacDowell Colony. In 1986, she received a New York Foundation for the Arts Fellowship, which enabled her to write the initial draft of *Mama*. The Before Columbus Foundation presented her with a National Book Award for *Mama*. In 1988, she won a prestigious National Endowment for the Arts Fellowship. She was also awarded a 1993 Matrix Award for Books by New York Women in Communications for *Waiting to Exhale*. These accolades have all paled in comparison to her tremendous financial success. Unfortunately, her activity as a teacher and critic has earned her no more recognition within the literary establishment than her art has.

Teaching and Scholarship

During the 1987–1988 academic year, McMillan was a visiting writer at the University of Wyoming, Laramie. In 1988, she accepted an associate professor position at the University of Arizona, Tucson, and still retains her tenure there. Since moving to Danville, California, she has also taught at Stanford University as a visiting professor. McMillan is a member of professional organizations for writers and artists, including PEN (The International Association of Poets, Playwrights, Editors, Essayists and Novelists), the Author's League, the Harlem Writers Guild, and Artists for a Free South Africa. In 1990, she served as a judge in the National Book Award for fiction competition and lobbied successfully to have the award presented to Charles Johnson for his novel *Middle Passage*. The last black man to win this award was Ralph Ellison, who received it for *Invisible Man* in 1953 (Fitchner). She has contributed essays to various periodicals, including *Callaloo, Esquire, Essence*, and *Other Voices*. McMillan has also written reviews for the *New York Times Book Review*, the *Atlanta Constitution*, and the *Philadelphia Inquirer*.

McMillan conceived the idea for *Breaking Ice: An Anthology of Contemporary African-American Fiction* (1990) after reading a collection of short stories that did not include any black or Third World writers. This omission angered her so much that she asked her publisher, Viking, to help her correct what she saw as the industry's neglect of black writers. From almost three hundred submissions, she selected fifty-seven stories representing emerging or unpublished authors as well as seasoned writers (Malinowski 423). Author Joyce Carol Oates, who reviewed the collection for the *Washington Post Book World*, praised McMillan's critical judgment in selecting such a uniformly high quality of submissions. She said, "one could hardly distinguish between the categories [of writers] in terms of originality, depth of vision, and command of the language" (quoted in Malinowski 423). Nevertheless, McMillan's activities as a teacher and as a critic have remained largely unrecognized by the literary establishment. Worse, McMillan's professional credentials are all too often overlooked when critics discuss the merits of her work, despite the fact that she is an artist who has invested an impressive amount of time and energy into mastering her craft.

Commercial Success

McMillan's skill has always garnered her a favorable reception in the marketplace. Thanks to her own promotional efforts, the first printing of *Mama* had sold out before it was released. Simon & Schuster eventually paid $81,000 for the paperback rights and released a Pocket Books edition in 1994. *Mama*'s paperback sales alone have totaled more than 1.2 million copies (O'Brien 124).

McMillan has also garnered many favorable reviews in the mass media. *Mama* received notices in the *New York Times Book Review, Publishers Weekly,* and the *New Yorker,* three of the most influential and respected forums in the publishing world. For a black female writer to have her debut novel reviewed by these publications was quite an achievement. Better still, all three reviews were positive, praising McMillan's way with dialect, her realism, the powerful characterization of Mildred Peacock, and the humorous perspective that keeps Mildred and her family from being helpless victims.

Disappearing Acts built on McMillan's earlier success. She had some trouble selling the proposal to Houghton Mifflin, the publisher of *Mama,* which wanted to see a completed manuscript before bidding on the book. Editors also objected that Zora's voice was too "white." McMillan refused to compromise her vision of the character, insisting that "some of us [African Americans] have been to college" (Smith 50). Instead, she instructed her agent to shop the project around. Viking purchased the novel two days after receiving the proposal. Clearly McMillan had learned early on how to negotiate in the publishing industry.

Nevertheless, reviewers such as Valerie Sayers of the *New York Times Book Review* echoed the criticisms McMillan had received from her editors. Sayers stated that "Zora's voice, though generally likable, has a bland quality (Franklin's son says she 'talk like white people')." However, like most of the novel's critics, Sayers appreciated McMillan's achievement in characterizing Franklin through his voice: "The miracle is that Ms. McMillan takes the reader so deep into this man's head—and makes what goes on there so complicated—that his story becomes not only comprehensible but affecting" (Sayers 8). Once again, critics remarked and praised McMillan's realism, and, as they had with *Mama,* they frequently compared her to Alice Walker. Perhaps this was because Walker was the most commercially successful black female writer of the time. Yet, ironically, these comparisons also implicitly attributed some literary merit to McMillan's work. Additionally, the *Washington Post Book World* reviewer praised the novel as "one of the few . . . to contain rounded, sympathetic portrayals of black men and to depict relationships between black men and black women as something more than the relationship between victimizer and victim, oppressor and oppressed" (David Nicholson, quoted in Malinowski 422). Yet reviewers such as Sayers failed to understand McMillan's revisionist relationship to popular romance and condemned her plot and descriptive prose for reflecting some romance conventions.

Despite these criticisms, *Disappearing Acts* was quickly optioned for a film, and McMillan wrote a screenplay based on the novel for Metro-Goldwyn-Mayer. This version of the story failed to materialize on the big screen, but Home Box Office has picked up the option and is currently producing an adaptation of *Disappearing Acts* for television. Simon & Schuster released a Pocket Books edition in 1993, which has sold more than 1.2 million copies to date (O'Brien 124).

The publication of *Waiting to Exhale* marked an important turning point in McMillan's career and in the history of African American popular fiction. The novel cracked the *New York Times* best-seller list. It opened in the number eleven slot on the *Publishers Weekly* hardcover fiction best-seller list on June 1, 1992. By October 5, it had reached the number one position. As late as April 5, 1993, *Waiting to Exhale* was still holding the fourteenth position on the *Publishers Weekly* list (BookWire). Altogether, *Waiting to Exhale* stayed on the list for forty-three weeks. By 1996, readers had purchased 650,000 hardcover copies (O'Brien 124). Following this phenomenal success, Simon & Schuster paid $2.64 million for the paperback rights, the second highest price ever paid at that time. The Pocket Books edition was released in May 1993. Meanwhile, Twentieth Century Fox won the bidding war for the screen rights, paying $1 million for the privilege of making the novel into a movie. It also put the project promptly into production. Many new readers purchased the book after seeing the film, which was released in December 1995. Within the first two months of 1996, total sales for hardcover and paperback copies of *Waiting to Exhale* had exceeded 1.75 million (O'Brien 124).

Both the novel and the film were widely reviewed. Above all, critics praised the vernacular voice McMillan used to narrate the story. Reviewers also appreciated McMillan's humor and the palpable bonds she portrayed among the four female friends. Susan Isaacs of the *New York Times Book Review* recognized McMillan's debt to other novels about female friendship such as *The Group* by Mary McCarthy, *The Best of Everything* by Rona Jaffe, and *Best Friends* by Consuelo S. Baehr. Frances Stead Sellers of the *Times Literary Supplement* similarly categorized *Waiting to Exhale* as glitzy women's fiction for an overlooked audience—the new black middle class. She, like most of McMillan's other critics, saw this commercial orientation as incompatible with true literary merit. In accordance with Sellers, some critics found the plot superficial and the characters shallow. In particular, McMillan drew fire for male bashing. Indeed, as had been the case with Alice Walker's *The Color Purple*, the media spotlight that focused first on the book and then on the film reignited an old controversy about the role of feminism in the black community.

One of the earliest and most thorough explorations of this topic appears in the May/June 1979 issue of the *Black Scholar*. The previous issue had featured an essay by Robert Staples entitled "The Myth of Black Macho: A Response to Angry Black Feminists." Staples's essay raised so much controversy that the editors devoted the next issue of the journal to a "Reader's Forum on Black Male/Female Relationships." The contributors came from a whole spectrum of academic disciplines and expressed a wide variety of opinions; however, one point of consensus was that the white-controlled media lionize works like Ntozake Shange's *for colored girls who have considered suicide/when the rainbow is enuf* (1977) and Michele Wallace's *Black Macho* (1979) because they can be made to fit the stereotypes about abusive black men and victimized black women with which the mass audience is comfortable. The publication and subsequent screen adaptation of Walker's *The Color Purple* touched off another round in the debate. This time, participants expressed even more suspicion and dissatisfaction with the white-controlled media. Protestors picketed the movie, charging that it misrepresented black men. Meanwhile, Ishmael Reed, McMillan's teacher, complained of similar institutional prejudice in the publishing industry because his work was not receiving the kind of media attention that was focused on Alice Walker and Toni Morrison.

Almost a decade later, when the film version of *Waiting to Exhale* appeared in December 1995, the controversy over feminism in the black community still had not been resolved. The April 1996 issue of *Ebony* magazine included a symposium debating "Was the Movie Fair to Black Men and Black Women?" just as Edward M. Jackson, one of the few critics to offer a scholarly analysis of McMillan's work, had similarly chosen to focus on "Images of Black Males in Terry McMillan's *Waiting to Exhale*" for a 1993 *MAWA Review* issue after the book had been released.

The controversy over *Waiting to Exhale* fueled interest in McMillan's work. Thus, Viking was so confident readers would like *How Stella Got Her Groove Back* that it released an initial printing of 800,000 hardcover copies—an unprecedented first printing for a novel by a black woman writer. *Stella* shot to the top of the *Publishers Weekly* hardcover fiction best-seller list in its first week. It remained on the list for twenty-one weeks, averaging fifth position during its stay (BookWire). Twentieth Century Fox purchased the film rights for $2 million and cast Angela Bassett, who had anchored *Waiting to Exhale* with her performance as Bernadine, in the role of Stella. McMillan's departure from social realism in the novel has confused many reviewers, however, and there is a sharp split between those who accept the novel as a pleasurable romantic fantasy and those who find the plot far-fetched and unrealistic. Most critics have continued to praise McMillan's vernacular voice and her flair for dialogue, but several have objected that the stream-of-consciousness narration is awkward and difficult to read in places. The novel has generated the most interest for its autobiographical basis and the unconventional older woman/younger man relationship it depicts. Since McMillan reportedly drafted the book in a little over one month, critics have also tended to regard it as an interim offering that serves to satisfy McMillan's loyal fans until she can produce a more substantial new work.

The film version of *How Stella Got Her Groove Back* also received mixed reviews. Audiences enjoyed the lush Jamaican landscapes and the lavish designer interiors. They also appreciated Angela Bassett and Taye Diggs' well-toned physiques. Critics found the plot too superficial and objected to the happily-ever-after ending. At best they described the film as a beautiful fantasy.

Academic Criticism

Academic critics have been curiously silent about McMillan's work despite the milestone achievement she represents in African American publishing history. Aside from Jackson's essay, the Modern Language Association (MLA) bibliography lists only one other article that refers to

McMillan's work. This essay, "Don't Worry, Be Buppie: Black Novelists Head for the Mainstream," by Thulani Davis, appeared in the May 1990 *Village Voice Literary Supplement,* a respectable publication but not a scholarly periodical. In contrast, the MLA bibliography lists twenty-eight citations about the works of Chinese American writer Amy Tan, who has enjoyed comparable success in the popular marketplace. Fortunately, Rita B. Dandrige's essay "Debunking the Motherhood Myth in Terry McMillan's *Mama,*" which appeared in the June 1998 issue of the *CLA Journal,* marks a new critical interest in McMillan's work.

Mass media reviewers have frequently placed McMillan in company with Alice Walker, Gloria Naylor, and even Toni Morrison. Academic critics have been more hesitant to do so. Margaria Fichtner quotes Linda Strong-Leek of Florida International University saying, "Most of my colleagues don't teach her, and in the academic community she's not really considered . . . I don't want to say a writer, but, you know, she's not considered an Alice Walker" (Fichtner). Academic critics question the merits of McMillan's form, and many regard her work as disturbingly apolitical. Her descriptions of affluent middle-class lifestyles seem to avoid addressing the political and social issues that African American literature has traditionally emphasized. Elizabeth Nunez, head of the National Black Writers Conference, has expressed concern that McMillan's example will lead other black writers to conclude, "Hey, if you want to get popular, then stop writing literature that is race centered" (quoted in Leland). McMillan, however, shows her disdain for such criticism by spoofing it in her most recent novel, *How Stella Got Her Groove Back*:

> after reading like the first fifty or sixty pages I don't know what all the hoopla is about and why everybody thinks she's such a hot writer because her shit is kind of weak when you get right down to it and this book here has absolutely no literary merit whatsoever at least none that I can see and she uses entirely too much profanity. (60)

McMillan told Cassandra Spratling in a May 22, 1996, interview, "I put it [the above passage] in to let them know that I know what they say and I don't care. . . . What I've done, and what I will do, is write what I feel like writing. I can only hope that people like what I do."

Pioneering a New Genre

Whatever status the literary establishment ultimately accords Terry McMillan's work, in the annals of popular fiction she will be remembered as the foremother of an entirely new genre. Indeed, as Malcolm Jones, Jr., pointed out in his 1996 *Newsweek* article "Successful Sisters: Faux Terry Is Better Than No Terry," McMillan has gone innovative popular fiction writers like James Michener and Tom Clancy one better by creating an entirely new audience to go with her genre. McMillan may not have single-handedly created the audience of black women readers who fervently support her work, but she was the first to recognize their hunger for fiction that represented their lives.

Publishers Weekly reports that expenditures for books rose 26 percent in African American households between 1988 and 1991, while white households purchased 3 percent fewer books in the same period. African American publishers and bookstores have also grown at an exponential rate. Between 1968 and 1994, the number of African American publishers jumped from seven to seventy-five. The number of African American bookstores increased even more dramatically, from ten to three hundred (Mitchell-Powell 33). Tina McElroy Ansa, whose first novel, *Ugly Ways* (1993), sold 92,000 hardcover copies in the wake of the *Waiting to Exhale* phenomenon, says, "I've never seen black people read the way they've been reading. They're hungry . . . they're mad with us because we don't have new books" (quoted in Stovall 42).

Inspiring a New School of Writers

The need to fill the demand created by Terry McMillan's success has opened doors for many other writers. Meanwhile, she has not only tapped into a new readership, she has inspired a whole new generation of authors. Among the wave of new writers following in McMillan's footsteps is her younger sister Rosalyn. Rosalyn McMillan's agent sold her finished novel *Knowing* to Warner Books in a five-figure deal without realizing that her client was the sister of superstar Terry McMillan (Hubbard, April 1, 1996).

McMillan's literary descendants extend beyond her blood kin to include a whole raft of new voices *Essence* magazine has identified as

"Terry's Children" (74). Whereas Bebe Moore Campbell, Connie Briscoe, Tina McElroy Ansa, and E. Lynn Harris are contemporaries whose works have been buoyed by McMillan's success, "Terry's Children" are younger writers deliberately extending the urban contemporary mode she developed. Readers have "inhaled" the following novels in between installments from McMillan: *Tryin' to Sleep in the Bed You Made* by Virginia DeBerry and Donna Grant; *Nothing but the Rent* by Sharon Mitchell; *Behind Closed Doors* by Kimberla Lawson Roby; *Caught Up in the Rapture* and *Li'l Mama's Rules* by Sheneska Jackson; and *Good Hair* and *The Itch* by Benilde Little. Significantly, this roster also includes upcoming male writers such as Eric Jerome Dickey, author of *Sister, Sister* and *Friends and Lovers*, and Franklin White, author of *Fed Up with the Family*. These "brothers," like the "sisters," chronicle life in black middle-class communities with particular emphasis on interpersonal relationships.

Trey Ellis, author of the satire *Platitudes*, categorizes these writers as members of a "New Black Aesthetic." Characteristically, these writers represent the lives and loves of middle-class African Americans. References to contemporary popular culture provide the context in which the characters move. Meanwhile, detailed descriptions of the characters' material possessions and opulent lifestyles satisfy the wish-fulfillment fantasies of the readership. Most importantly, African American characters and their worldview occupy the narrative center of these works. The white world is either markedly absent or pushed to the margins of the fictional space.

The more traditional African American critical establishment views these novels as improbable or even dangerously frivolous because they do not grapple with racial tensions the way African American literature had in the past. Yet McMillan has commented that in dealing with everything in life from the perspective of race, a lot of earlier writers "were appealing to a white audience, hoping they would say, 'OK now we understand you people more. Thanks for sharing' " (Leland). McMillan and her followers are secure in the knowledge that, for the first time, they are speaking *en famille* to a primary audience of African American readers. Participating in this imagined print community frees the writers to air family secrets as well as to tell family jokes. At the same time, these novels are not devoid of political content. E. Lynn Harris's works constitute a sermon on tolerance which counters traditional religious condemnations of homosexuality. For example, Sheneska Jackson's *Lil' Mama's Rules* is a cautionary tale targeting the group most at risk for

HIV infection—African American women. Further, all these novels continue the ongoing struggle to inject positive representations of blacks into the popular American imagination.

African American writers have traditionally drawn on a rich body of oral literature in addition to the oral and written canons of Western literature to shape their creative works. McMillan's novels stand at an important juncture in the evolution of African American literature because they provide a body of popular fiction to nourish the creative imagination along with the oral traditions. As a young girl shelving books in the public library, McMillan was touched by the Brontë sisters, whose enduring works sprout from a similar combination of literary predecessors, folktales, and popular romance novels. As a mature writer, McMillan has chosen to address the mass audience rather than the literary establishment. She may never produce a *Wuthering Heights*, but her way with dialect, her insights into relationships, and her ability to translate the oral culture of her primary audience into print will provide the seedbed for future literary masterpieces.

2

Literary Contexts

Scholars and critics may disagree about the literary merit of McMillan's works, but her status as the first best-selling African American popular fiction writer endows her career with sociocultural interest. What factors have made it possible for an African American woman to succeed as a popular fiction writer at this juncture in American history? What do her millions of readers of all races find to identify with in her stories? And what can the themes in McMillan's novels, which have captured the popular imagination, reveal about widely held values and beliefs of her time? This chapter demonstrates that McMillan's work is rooted in both literary and vernacular traditions of African American storytelling and argues that McMillan is particularly innovative in the creative writing techniques she uses to synthesize these two traditions into a powerful aesthetic vision.

WOMEN'S POPULAR FICTION

It is important to read McMillan's work in the context of the twentieth-century romance boom for several reasons. First of all, the economic clout of women's fiction helped make it possible for publishers to risk investing in black female popular fiction writers like Terry McMillan and Bebe Moore Campbell. Romance novels account for more than 40 percent of all paperback books sold in the United States. Although the genre is commonly dismissed by most reviewers and critics as "trash," it is the bread and butter of the national book chains. This means there is a large body of women readers frequenting these shops to get their regular romance "fix." Indeed, when Janice Radway set out to interview a community of romance readers, she relied on the proprietor of a bookshop to help her contact women who might be willing to participate. While in the store, the romance reader is likely to purchase other genres of books as well. For example, women purchase at least 60 percent of all mystery novels. Thus, it is reasonable to assume some overlap in fans of the genres, and the hard-core romance fan may simultaneously be a voracious and omnivorous reader supporting a wide variety of writers and genres. Overall, women buy more books than men. What this spells is a large potential audience of women readers who can relate to McMillan's work, even if it does not fit the conventions of romance or other genre fiction, because relationships are still the central component of her novels.

Feminist Views of Romance

In the 1980s, some feminist scholars like Tania Modleski and Janice Radway began to study romance fiction because it was a genre written and read almost entirely by women. Feminist scholars argued that romance was devalued precisely because it was a female-dominated form. They were especially interested in the values romance readers and writers communicated to each other as the form evolved. Indeed, one of the most striking observations feminist scholars made was that the books did not just repeat the same story over and over. Not only was there a great variety of subgenres and innovative plots within the general romance category, the conventions of the genre as a whole were in a continuous process of change that reflected the radical changes in women's post—World War II roles in society.

Romances of the early 1960s usually featured virginal heroines in their late teens or early twenties. The heroine was typically orphaned or separated from her own social network. The hero tended to be much older than the heroine (ten to fifteen years), and he was always much wealthier and much more powerful. Publishers like Harlequin issued guidelines to their authors instructing them to use third-person limited omniscient narration, thus restricting the narrative to the heroine's point of view.

Since the form did not permit readers to access the hero's thoughts, he remained a silent mystery to them as well as to the heroine, who spent most of the book trying to understand his seemingly irrational responses to her. The heroine often could not tell if the hero was a dangerous enemy or her champion and protector until the end of the book, when he made his requisite confession of love. Readers and heroines alike were then reassured that their prince charmings never really meant to hurt them. Feminist response to these romances initially deplored them as mass-produced fantasies that brainwashed women into accepting their second-class status in society. At the same time, however, the sexual revolution was raising important questions about women's fantasies and desires.

In 1972, Nancy Friday published *My Secret Garden*, a groundbreaking collection of sexual fantasies contributed by women all over the United States. Up until this time, researchers had either assumed that women did not have erotic fantasies or had not considered the subject important enough for serious study. Friday's book helped explode lingering Victorian notions that good women didn't really enjoy sex and didn't really think about it except when approached by a man. In this same period, women were exploring *Our Bodies Ourselves* (1970) and discovering their orgasmic capacity.

In the midst of this growing sexual assertiveness, women readers were also supporting an unprecedented boom in paperback romance novels. Paradoxically, the best-selling titles in the 1970s were historical pieces set in time periods when women had almost no political or economic power and a woman's social status depended on the man (father or husband) to whom she belonged. These novels became known as "bodice rippers" because they were much more sexually explicit than earlier romances had been. Instead of experiencing a delicious kiss or a mystical wedding night at the end of the story, heroines in the bodice rippers were regularly ravished by the hero. Some feminist critics objected to these books as a romanticization of rape, but readers identified strongly with the heroine's powerlessness as a woman in a rigidly patriarchal society. Unlike the sweet virgins of earlier romances, the heroines of the bodice rippers were notoriously feisty. No matter how many times they were humiliated for being female, they kept fighting, and eventually they tamed the savage beast in the hero through the power of love. Readers and heroines understood that the hero was so overcome by his passion that he could not restrain himself enough to court the woman of his dreams in a gentlemanly manner. Indeed, for women who had been taught "nice girls don't," the hero's uncontrollable passion allowed them to be swept away by their own desire without feeling guilty. Thus, the bodice rippers, like the rape fantasies Nancy Friday collected, enabled women to express their desires within the limits of their socially pre-scribed roles. Feminist critics of romance objected that this mechanism served to perpetuate the status quo precisely because it allowed women to accommodate themselves to it. Nevertheless, romance continued to evolve along with women's role in society.

The Changing Roles of Women

By 1980, over 50 percent of all women were in the paid workforce, and 38 percent of all mothers with children under one year old worked outside the home (Taeuber 72, 112). Romance reflected these trends in several ways. Heroines became older and more experienced. They were no longer required to be virgins, although the genre still celebrated the romantic, monogamous union as the highest sexual ideal for women. More significantly, instead of depending on the hero for economic support, more heroines had successful careers or owned profitable busi-nesses, and many plots reflected contemporary women's dilemmas over balancing their careers with marriage and family life. Time to pursue their own interests and indulge their own whims became a precious commodity for many women. Advertisers recognized this need and sold their products to women as brief but refreshing reprieves from the de-mands of their daily lives. Harlequin aired television ads touting their books as an affordable indulgence.

Meanwhile, the image of the hero within the idealized world of these novels was changing to meet women's desire for a sensitive, egalitarian partner. Romance heroes knew how to cook gourmet meals, and they volunteered to do housework. As writers like Laura Kinsale began to experiment with incorporating the male point of view into their stories, heroes' thoughts and motivations were more accessible, and the heroes themselves seemed more in touch with their own emotions than the strong silent types who had come before. These novels show that in the midst of an often antagonistic tension between the sexes in the public sphere, romance fans still wanted to communicate with men and under-stand their perspective on the changing world in which men and women found themselves.

By the time McMillan published *Disappearing Acts*, the pendulum was beginning to swing back the other way. Romance fiction saw the return of the masterful alpha male. Romance writers like Jayne Ann Krentz have argued that the stronger, more confident heroines of the 1990s needed bolder men as partners. Romance novels had also grown progressively more explicit in their representations of erotic love, and readers seemed to appreciate passionate lovers more than sensitive helpmates (at least in their fantasy lives). The alpha male hero, however, was a modern warrior who used his masculine power to protect his loved ones in an increasingly dangerous world. His authority derived from a strong sense of self rather than from socially prescribed dominance over "inferior" beings. If the heroine "submitted" to the hero, it was in recognition of the protection he offered springing from a loving need to safeguard her best interests. Meanwhile, the alpha male hero learned to defer to the heroine's good judgment and humanitarian moral values.

McMillan and African American Popular Romance

The rise of women's popular fiction is one factor that has made McMillan's phenomenal success possible. Simultaneously, McMillan's success has helped awaken publishers to the viability of African American women's popular fiction. In particular, McMillan's work has paved the way for mainstream distribution and marketing of African American romance lines such as Arabesque and Indigo. Thus, the second reason for reading McMillan's work in the context of the romance boom is to develop a greater appreciation for the African American cultural inflection she brings to her representations of black love.

It is fairly uncommon for romance publishers to incur the extra expense of including photos of novice authors on the back jacket. Yet, almost from the beginning, Arabesque used this strategy to authenticate the African American voice in its novels. Arabesque writers have evoked black middle-class life by endowing heroes and heroines with degrees from historically black colleges, by making them members of African American fraternities or sororities, and by setting the stories in affluent black neighborhoods familiar to readers who have lived in Washington, D.C., Atlanta, Chicago, or other urban centers with a strong black middle class. Arabesque writers have also introduced into their plotlines some subjects of particular concern to black communities, such as the ravages of drug-related crime and violence, environmental racism, and the activities of white supremacist hate groups. Even when Arabesque writers attempt a romance set in the antebellum period, however, the conventions of the genre require that the author create a microcosmic community in which the hero and heroine can function as autonomous individuals, free to commit themselves to loving each other as whole human beings.

African American historical romances regularly depict romance between free people of color during the antebellum period, but to date, no popular romance writer has published a love story in which the hero and heroine are both slaves. In contrast, *Disappearing Acts* foregrounds the impact of economic and political disempowerment on an African American couple struggling to love each other in an environment that consistently attacks their ability to love themselves. Not until *How Stella Got Her Groove Back* did McMillan offer her readers a fairy-tale happy ending, and even then, she handled the genre in a most innovative way. In other words, McMillan works within genres familiar to readers of popular women's fiction, but her original approach to these forms draws on traditions that have developed in African American literature.

THE IMAGINED PRINT COMMUNITY

McMillan's readings regularly draw over one thousand people. She estimates that African Americans make up 90 percent of these audiences (Daniel 20). Thus, it is clear that while her work has the power to cross over into the mainstream market and attract readers from all ethnic backgrounds, the core audience purchasing her books is solidly black. African-American musicians have always been able to count on this kind of support from the black community. Until McMillan's time, however, African American writers had to assume that the majority of the book-buying public would be white. Even as late as 1983 Alice Walker told interviewer Claudia Tate for the latter's book *Black Women Writers at Work*, "We don't have a large black readership; I mean black people, generally speaking, don't read" (182).

Tate published this interview two years before the screen version of *The Color Purple*, before anyone had bothered to count all the copies of *The Color Purple* that accompanied black women commuting to and from work on buses and subway trains. Still, Walker's comments show keen insight into the relationship between black women writers and the black female audience: "Twentieth-century black women writers all seem to be much more interested in the black community, in intimate relationships, with the white world as a *backdrop*" (quoted in Tate 181). Walker saw this interest as progress over the situation of black women writers in the nineteenth century, who had to be concerned about what white readers would think. However, more than a decade later, McMillan and the school of African American popular fiction writers that is emerging in her wake are being dismissed as frivolous largely because they portray a network of relationships within a self-contained black community.

Walker also observed, "Black women instinctively feel a need to connect with their reading audience, to be direct, to build a readership for us all, but more than that, to build *independence*. None of us will survive except in very distorted ways if we have to depend on white publishers and white readers forever" (quoted in Tate 182). Walker's prediction that "the time has to come when the majority of black people, not just two or three, will want their own novels and poems, will want their own folk tales, will want their own folk songs, will want their own whatever" (183) has come true.

What Walker foresaw was the advent of a cultural nationalist consciousness that arises out of a phenomenon Benedict Anderson calls the "imagined community." Anderson's theory emphasizes that national or ethnic group identity is a collective fiction. His analysis focuses on the role of print media in shaping these fictions. African American music has always served as the primary vehicle for transmitting the collective African American consciousness and identity. McMillan's work marks the crystallization of an imagined print community among African Americans.

Slavery and African American Literacy

Although most of the African captives brought to the Americas as slaves came from oral cultures, some were Muslims who were already familiar with the concept of sacred writing. In the United States, slaveholders cited another sacred text—namely, Genesis (9:21–27)—as proof that the "sons of Ham" were cursed by God to be slaves for all eternity. Thus, in one sense, African American identity has always been a fiction rooted in print. Yet African Americans have continuously asserted their power to reinterpret sacred texts and create their own identity myths. As they embraced Christianity, African Americans identified with the enslaved Hebrews and took comfort in the belief that they would eventually be redeemed from bondage just as the Hebrews were delivered from Egypt. Although it was a crime to teach slaves to read, some were able to acquire the rudiments of literacy, and others were able to memorize many passages from the Bible after hearing them read aloud at church services. After emancipation, African Americans of all ages expressed a keen interest in learning to read. Many cited the desire to read the Bible as one of their strongest motivations. Some wanted to understand the message of the Gospels better and deepen their own faith. Others had always found great spiritual solace in hearing the Scriptures read aloud. They wanted to be able to provide this comfort for themselves. For many others, however, the ability to read the Bible would at last give them the power to reevaluate the interpretation of Scripture white slaveholders had proposed.

A rudimentary imagined print community has therefore existed among African Americans since the nineteenth century. Bible study groups have been an important spiritual and social institution for generations, especially for those who had less education and could not easily read the Scriptures for themselves. African American communities were also interested in secular events. The black press has a long and distinguished history because "all the news that's fit to print" often did not include events of interest to the black community. The editorial perspective of the black press also reflected experiences and values with which black readers could more readily identify. Illiteracy was not a barrier to participating in intellectual discussions in the black community. Newspapers were frequently read aloud on porches, in poolrooms, in barbershops, and in beauty parlors. Indeed, the wisdom gleaned from life experience almost always carried more authority than the printed word. Even when more educated groups formed literary societies, they usually grew out of church congregations or women's clubs. Literary pursuits were therefore aligned with a philosophy of spiritual evolution and racial uplift.

African American Reading Groups and the Purpose of Literature

Continuing in this tradition of racial uplift, African American reading groups are a burgeoning social phenomenon in the late twentieth century. Some are based on college campuses, some are hosted by black-owned bookstores, some are affiliated with churches or professional organizations, while others draw their membership from informal social networks. African American book discussion groups also exhibit great diversity in their membership profiles and in their selection choices. Reading groups can also be focused on a specific genre such as poetry or romance. The discussion itself may be scholarly and passionate, or it might serve as only the pretext for a pleasant social gathering. Despite this great diversity, however, African American reading groups are all heirs to particular expectations about the process of reading that developed in the African American community even before emancipation.

One of these expectations is that literature serves a functional purpose. This belief is consonant with both African and African American philosophy about the role of all arts in society. African Americans are accustomed to turning to "the word" for spiritual solace. Regardless of its secular orientation, African American popular fiction continues to serve this purpose. McMillan consciously tries to offer readers a little optimism and hope, if only through her humor.

Although African Americans live within a print culture, they still value "the word" as an oral experience. Hence, book tours and public readings have become an important part of the connection between writers and readers in the imagined African American print community. Receiving "the word" in performance allows for a communal interpretation of the text. Members of African American book clubs who attend a public reading and then discuss the work among themselves are engaged in the same process as generations of African Americans who received "the word" from the preacher on Sunday and then met to discuss the Scripture in Bible study groups during the week.

This process of communal interpretation is especially important to African American readers because there is an ongoing struggle in U.S. society over the nature of reality. Are African Americans the accursed descendants of Canaan, destined for second-class citizenship? Or are they God's chosen people in the New World, whose sufferings will ultimately illuminate the path of righteousness for all mankind? This yet-unresolved clash of perspectives has made the power to read and interpret the truth fundamental in defining African American consciousness. The power to write or attest to one's truth in print has assumed even more significance.

African Americans Writing Truth

African American critic Henry Louis Gates, Jr., has noted that Enlightenment notions of reason and humanity codified writing as the highest symbol of human beings' capacity to reason. Consequently, Gates argues that, for African Americans, the act of writing is inevitably a trial by which the author seeks to prove his or her worth as a reasoning human being. McMillan names the protagonist of her first novel, Freda, after the most famous African American to prove his humanity in this way—Frederick Douglass. Douglass escaped from slavery, painstakingly educated himself, and became a powerful orator and writer. In his celebrated autobiography, Douglass impressed on his readers' minds the conclusion that literacy was the surest path to freedom. His own life became a testament to this truism.

Like many fictional protagonists, Freda is in some measure an alter ego for her creator. Yet she follows in her famous namesake's footsteps and becomes a journalist rather than a fiction writer like McMillan. Nevertheless, she shares with her creator as well as with her namesake the desire to expose truth to a mass audience. Thus, McMillan's work follows in Douglass's tradition by seeking to extend the liberating power of written narrative to a vernacular audience of black readers.

DOUBLE CONSCIOUSNESS

African American writers have always lamented the double burden of having to prove their worth as human beings while at the same time trying to represent their own truths through art. It was W.E.B. Du Bois, however, who most clearly articulated the difficulties of this position in his 1903 meditation on *The Souls of Black Folk*. In the very first chapter of this influential work, Du Bois developed a metaphor of the American Negro as a "seventh son" among the races of man, born behind a veil that gave him special insight into the peculiarities of American institutions but no true self-consciousness. Du Bois argued that Negro identity was based in a kind of "double-consciousness," which he defined as "the sense of always looking at one's self through the eyes of others" (38). He further asserted that all American Negroes longed for acceptance as Americans but were reluctant to give up their African-ness.

In Du Bois's estimation, artists were most profoundly affected by the internal contradictions double consciousness created:

> The innate love of harmony and beauty that set the ruder souls of his people a-dancing and a-singing raised but confusion and doubt in the soul of the black artist: for the beauty

revealed to him was the soul-beauty of a race which his larger audience despised, and he could not articulate the message of another people. (39)

Double consciousness led African American writers to censor both the form and content of their works. Terry McMillan is the first African American writer to manifest such complete confidence that a large reading audience will identify with her unadulterated African American truth. A brief examination of the techniques her pioneering predecessors have used to bring African American writing to this point should therefore prove useful for better appreciating her achievement.

Frame and Dialect

Novelist and critic John Edgar Wideman has suggested that the best approach to tracing the development of African American literature is to examine the evolution of the "frame and dialect" paradigm (Wideman 34–37). Most African captives were not given formal instruction in the English language after they were enslaved. Thus, African Americans in slave communities developed a dialect that combined English with the grammatical structures from various African languages. When African Americans began to write their own stories, they discovered that there was already a body of literature defining the African American voice in print. What slaveholders and visitors to the South had written about blacks was the accepted reality.

By the eighteenth century, playwrights were already using black speech as comic relief in their stage productions (Wideman 34). After the Civil War, a school of white southern writers, which included Joel Chandler Harris and Thomas Nelson Page, created a romanticized portrait of the plantation system in the antebellum South. The black dialect they invented made the black characters appear childish and intellectually deficient, but this stereotype soon took the tenor of reality in the popular American imagination. Many African Americans did speak nonstandard dialects of English, and African American writers wanted to represent black speech in ways that were authentic and expressive of an African American worldview. Yet what white publishers and readers expected from black writers was a stylized language that would reconfirm their white supremacist prejudices. Some gifted writers like Paul Laurence Dunbar managed to make black dialect into an eloquent literary form. Dunbar's dialect poetry was tremendously popular. But his publishers and readers would not accept anything else from him. Indeed, most did not believe that blacks were capable of writing literary prose. The burden of proving otherwise further handicapped generations of African American writers.

Black dialect had originally entered into American literature within the narrative frames provided by white writers. Black characters were never the central narrators of these stories. Instead, their dialect speech appeared in dialogue passages framed by a white narrator's voice. Wideman notes that this frame "implies a linguistic hierarchy, the dominance of one language variety over all others. This linguistic subordination extends naturally to the dominance of one version of reality over others" (36). Here Wideman addresses a crucial point, for the frame and dialect model not only dictated how black writers should express themselves, it also limited what they could say. Some topics and points of view fell outside the realm of what white audiences were willing to accept as reality. Wideman hails Charles Chesnutt for his genius in manipulating the frame and dialect model to present a more realistic portrait of black life.

The Contributions of Charles Chesnutt

Charles Waddell Chesnutt was light enough to pass for white but chose to be identified as a black man. He tried to use his writing to win a hearing for the black man's point of view. For several years at the turn of the century, he was remarkably successful in doing so. A series of short stories he published in the *Atlantic Monthly* appeared in a collection entitled *The Conjure Woman* in 1899. Chesnutt published four more works of fiction, *The Wife of His Youth and Other Stories of the Color Line* (1899), *The House Behind the Cedars* (1900), *The Marrow of Tradition* (1901), and *The Colonel's Dream* (1905), then turned his attention exclusively to his legal stenography business.

In *The Conjure Woman* stories, he followed the tradition of using a white narrator to serve as the "frame." This character was a northern white man named John who had settled on a former plantation in North Carolina after the Civil War. John employs an old black man named Uncle Julius as his coachman. Julius takes over as the central narrator of each chapter as he recounts his stories of life on the plantation "befo' de wah." By juxtaposing John's formal English with Julius's broad dialect, Chesnutt sets the two versions of reality in sharp contrast. He intensifies this conflict by weaving many elements of African American folk magic into Julius's stories. The black man's tales are frequently improbable. Yet he is able to use his storytelling to manipulate John just as Chesnutt used his own storytelling to manipulate his white audience into entertaining his point of view.

One of the realities Chesnutt successfully manipulated his readers into confronting was the tragic impact the slave system had on African American loving couples. His short story "Po Sandy" is one of the first literary representations of love between a black man and a black woman. In the story, a conjure woman named Tenie turns her partner into a pine tree so that he can stay near her instead of forever having to be at his master's beck and call. There is no space for Tenie and Sandy to love each other outside the realm of conjure, but even Tenie's supernatural power is not great enough to prevail against the brutality of the slave system. In the horrifying conclusion to the tale, Sandy the tree gets chopped down and sawed into planks while Tenie looks on in anguish. Chesnutt skillfully uses the "hoodoo" conceit of a human taking on the form of a tree to convey the emotional horror of such occurrences without having to confront his readers with the literal reality that slaves experienced—the reality of witnessing loved ones being whipped, tortured, or even murdered. Conjuring has subsequently become a trope that many African American writers have used to express a vision of reality that falls outside the experience of the mainstream readership. Yet the surest sign that McMillan envisions an audience that shares her point of view is the fact that she does not use the conjure conceit or any other forms of "metareality" in her work.

The Narrative Frame of Zora Neale Hurston

Zora Neale Hurston was another of the most important innovators in African American literature. Hurston was trained as an anthropologist and thus collected much knowledge of folklore and folk magic, which yielded rich and highly metaphorical systems of imagery in her fiction. Even more importantly, however, she relocated the black dialect voice within an African American narrative frame. While Hurston was still dependent on white patrons, publishers, and readers, her experience growing up in an all-black town enabled her to imagine a black audience for her stories. She set all of her novels except the last one in all-black communities. Her master work, *Their Eyes Were Watching God*, takes place in the all-black town of Eatonville, Florida, as Janie tells her life adventures to her best friend, Phoeby. This 1937 novel marked one of the only attempts to represent black-on-black love since Chesnutt's

"Po Sandy" appeared at the turn of the century. Thus, Hurston's formal innovation also allowed her to address a theme that black writers had not often dared to present to the primarily white readership before.

Janie tells her story in an authentic black dialect voice to an implied community of black women. Since the publication of Hurston's inspired masterpiece, African American writers have gained ever more freedom to break the frame and dialect mold and use black speech as "the independent expression of a speech community rather than a shorthand for indicating Negro inferiority" (Wideman 36). Consequently, when Savannah begins speaking as the first-person narrator in the opening chapter of *Waiting to Exhale*, McMillan does not have to invent a sympathetic audience for her to address. Just as African American musicians have adapted European-derived musical instruments and forms to their own artistic ends, McMillan can use standard English and European-derived literary forms to express truths that grow out of African American lived experience. Her skill in translating black English dialect into print cements her relationship with her core African American audience. At the same time, this skill is a measure of McMillan's artistry. McMillan does not simply transcribe contemporary black vernacular speech. Instead, she captures an urban black vernacular style while conforming to the rules of standard English grammar and usage so that all audiences can comfortably engage with her prose.

McMillan claims literary descent from Hurston by naming the heroine of *Disappearing Acts* Zora. McMillan's Zora also reserves a special place on her bookshelf for *Their Eyes Were Watching God.* Yet, in between Hurston's novel and McMillan's, only a handful of other black writers attempted the black-on-black love plot. Among the few African American love stories published in this fifty-year gap are *The Flagellants* (1967) by Carlene Hatcher Polite, *If Beale Street Could Talk* (1974) by James Baldwin, *Say Jesus and Come to Me* (1982) by Ann Allen Shockley, and *Mama Day* (1988) by Gloria Naylor. The fact that McMillan chose the romance plot for her second novel reflects her innovative spirit.

Of the African American love stories mentioned above, none provides so much potential space for the loving couple to fulfill their commitment to each other as *Say Jesus and Come to Me*. Shockley's novel about a preacher and a blues singer unites the sacred and secular traditions of the African American performance aesthetic. Indeed, her ability to imaginatively heal the sacred/secular split heralds the advent of a readership that can comfortably share in fictional worlds that represent the full gamut of African American lived experience. McMillan has capitalized on the crystallization of this imagined print community by elaborating a blues aesthetic in her works.

TESTIFYIN'

McMillan's novels transcend traditional popular fiction categories. Clearly they are women's fiction. Clearly they focus on relationships. But her approach to telling these stories differs from the conventions of popular romance as well as from those of other genres of popular women's fiction. Further, she changes structural form from novel to novel and frequently experiments with narrative voice. What remains consistent throughout McMillan's work is its strong basis in her autobiographical experience. McMillan herself has said that she sees her novels as a chronicle of her spiritual growth; and in interviews, she has also commented on her desire to portray her characters' growth. These remarks provide some clues for classifying McMillan's fiction. For the imagined print community responds to her work in the way that African American communities have traditionally responded to an oral performance mode known as "testifyin'."

African American linguist Geneva Smitherman describes the act of testifyin' as telling the "truth" through "story." She says that within a "sacred" context, its subject matter includes "visions, prophetic experiences, the experience of being saved, and testimony to the power and goodness of God." However, within a "secular" context, its subject matter, she notes, is more down to earth: "blues changes caused by yo man or yo woman; experiences attesting to the racist power of the white oppressor; testimonial to the power of a gifted musician or singer." The point of testifyn', then, is to retell occurrences in a "lifelike fashion" and thereby to re-create "the spiritual reality for others who at that moment vicariously experience what the testifier has gone through." In other words, Smitherman finds that testifyin' goes beyond "plain and simple commentary" to become a "dramatic narration" and "a communal reenactment of one's feelings and experiences." Accordingly, she argues, "one's humanity is reaffirmed by the group and his or her sense of isolation diminished" (Smitherman 150).

McMillan uses autobiographical elements in her work the way that a blues singer would draw on her experiences to give a greater sense of emotional truth to her testimony about life. Given the African American community's historical investment in "telling the truth through stories,"

it is not surprising that autobiography has been one of the most important forms of African American literature since the early slave narratives.
Frederick Douglass wrote three versions of his journey from slavery to
freedom. More recently, Maya Angelou has published five volumes
chronicling her life.

Although Smitherman points out that testifyin' can occur in either a
sacred or a secular context, the early slave narratives were usually spon-
sored by Christian abolitionists. Consequently, African American writers
adopted the European-derived conventions of the spiritual autobiography. In this tradition, the slavery experience became a metaphor for the
bondage all human souls suffer until they renounce sin and accept Jesus
Christ as their savior. The deliverance from slavery and the experience
of salvation in the North (known as the Promised Land) completed the
metaphor of the religious conversion experience. African Americans
learned to manipulate the spiritual autobiography as an effective literary
form for telling their truth through story, but the Christian definition of
sin and evil did not fit the traditional African understanding of the problem of evil in the universe.

In traditional African cosmology, everything in nature is endowed
with spirit. Spirit is an energy which might be used positively or negatively but is neither good nor evil in and of itself. What is "good" for
one person might harm another. Further, "evil" might actually end up
producing positive results. Since evil is not a totalizing force, it can co-
exist with good in the same universe. In the Christian conception the
question of evil raises greater paradoxes. How can a just and benevolent
God have created evil or permitted its continued existence in the universe? The existence of evil in the Christian universe implies that either
God is not all powerful—otherwise evil would be eradicated—or God
is not purely good. Christian theologians explain that God's plan is beyond the comprehension of human beings and that almighty God has a
purpose for all things, even for evil. In the minds of the slaveholders,
this paradox became a system of symbolic oppositions in which white
(good) was bound to prevail over black (evil) just as the spirit would
ultimately redeem the flesh.

This system of thought was also foreign to traditional African cosmology. Africans did not regard the body as a vessel of sin. Therefore,
they did not see sexuality as inherently evil the way Puritan-influenced
whites did. Africans certainly did not regard their skin color as the mark
of the devil the way many Europeans did. In fact, in his study *Slave*

Religion, Albert J. Raboteau demonstrates that while many slaves accepted Christianity, they did not give up traditional African cosmology. As a result, in African American folk culture, the traditional African belief system has been divided between sacred and secular paradigms. Rather than existing in opposition to each other, these two traditions are experienced as complementary parts of a metaphysical whole.

Further, as Smitherman points out in her description of testifyin', the formal elements of sacred and secular performance are often interchangeable. Indeed, performers themselves can switch between the secular and sacred paradigms. For example, Thomas Dorsey, author of such lascivious blues songs as "It's Tight Like That," also composed the most famous African American gospel song, "Precious Lord." Many soul and rhythm and blues (R&B) singers, from Sam Cooke and Aretha Franklin to Whitney Houston and Toni Braxton, grew up singing in church. The black church regularly calls secular performers like Al Green back into the fold to continue their careers in the sacred tradition. African American communities may frown on performers like Little Richard who move from secular to sacred music and then "backslide" into the secular world again. Still, the "saints" getting "happy" in church on Sunday morning respond to the same forms that moved the "sinners" on Saturday night. The Saturday night sinners and the Sunday morning saints may even be the same people.

This interchange of sacred and secular forms is part of the shared reality in the African American community, but it is not part of the reality known to the high-culture publishing industry. The legacy of the spiritual autobiography forced black writers to rely on tropes like Chesnutt's conjure when they wanted to introduce aspects of the African American "secular" worldview into a literary work. African Americans have been narrating blues autobiographies as analogues of the written spiritual autobiographies as long as they have been singing the blues. But prior to McMillan's era and the crystallization of a book-buying African American public, there was not much space for blues autobiography in print. Several famous autobiographies have drawn extensively on the secular world, including Claude Brown's *Manchild in the Promised Land* (1965), Iceberg Slim's *Pimp: The Story of My Life* (1969), and the *Autobiography of Malcolm X* (1964). Yet, because these narrators ultimately claim redemption, these texts are still in the spiritual autobiography mode, even though they do not attribute redemption to a Christian conversion experience.

The centrality of redemption is not just a spiritual matter: it also defines a political stance. McMillan's work has been criticized as apolitical, and she has been attacked for failing to offer solutions for the social issues she does raise. As blues testimonials, however, McMillan's novels have their own political logic: "Unlike sacred music, the blues deals with a world where the inability to solve a problem does not necessarily mean that one can, or ought to, transcend it" (Williams 74). In partnership with her imagined print community, McMillan is carrying on the work of incorporating African American experience into the larger American understanding of reality. Up until her time, African American musicians had been the most successful in this endeavor because African American music flourished as a popular rather than a high-culture form. African American musicians could get a hearing without having to adopt the conventions of Western art music. Awareness of this history has led African American writers and literary critics to borrow continually from "the blues aesthetic." McMillan is extending this time-honored strategy.

THE BLUES AESTHETIC

By the 1980s, the "blues aesthetic" was a common term in the language of African American literary critics. African American poet Amiri Baraka (then LeRoi Jones) had published *Blues People* in 1963. His work, like that of African American cultural critic Albert Murray, asserted that the blues express African Americans' philosophy, moral values, and attitudes toward life. Blues forms exemplify African American definitions of beauty, and blues paradigms constitute African American definitions of the function of art in society.

African American literary critics had been searching for a language that would allow them to discuss the merits of African American literature as measured against the value system expressed in the texts rather than against the value system of the majority culture. Works like Calvin Hernton's introduction to *Understanding the New Black Poetry* and Houston A. Baker, Jr.'s *Blues, Ideology, and Afro-American Literature* enabled critics to argue that African American writers had a continuous relationship with an alternative African American "canon," which had been preserved in oral literature forms such as the blues. This school of critics also sought to demonstrate that African American writers consistently drew on musical forms and blues sensibility in order to translate African American experience into written forms. They tried to identify the traits of a distinctly African American literary voice by comparing the prose rhythms, imagery, and themes African American writers used to musical analogues.

Whereas the blues aesthetic has been used primarily as a tool for identifying differences between African American and European American cultural norms, McMillan's use of blues conventions may actually be the key to her novels' crossover appeal. In literature and the fine arts, African Americans have had to struggle against biases that held that blacks were incapable of meeting the aesthetic standards of the literary establishment. In popular culture, however, every musical form African Americans have created has found a crossover audience and has wielded profound influence on the development of all forms of American music. White audiences embraced the spirituals when they were arranged for concert performances by the Fisk Jubilee Singers and other African American choral groups. White artists donned blackface and performed their own versions of African American secular music in touring minstrel shows, which enjoyed immense popularity in the latter half of the nineteenth century. Minstrelsy, in turn, influenced vaudeville and American musical theater on stage and screen. At the turn of the century, ragtime composers like Scott Joplin sold hundreds of thousands of copies of sheet music for their works to a whole racial and ethnic spectrum of Americans. By the time the phonograph arrived, there was a white audience willing to surreptitiously order recordings of their favorite black blues singers from companies that produced separate lines of "race" records targeted at black consumers. King Oliver's Creole Jazz Band entertained black troops stationed in Europe during World War I. European appreciation for this music helped all Americans embrace jazz as their own indigenous musical form. After the war, white youth became so enamored of the "fascinatin' rhythms" black performers developed that the period of American history from World War I to the onset of the Great Depression is frequently referred to as the "Jazz Age."

Indeed, while African American music has often been disdained as a "low-life" form born of juke joints and dives (not to mention bordellos), this designation has only increased its appeal for several generations of white American teenagers. In the 1950s, disc jockey Alan Freed noticed that white teens were buying a lot of R&B records by black artists. He began airing a "rock and roll" show that featured this music. Soon there were white artists like Bill Haley and the Comets, Pat Boone, and Elvis Presley duplicating the R&B sound. In 1989, when *Disappearing Acts* hit the bookstores, there was a national controversy about the risqué lyrics in rap songs, but the "parental advisory" warning that was eventually placed on CDs with explicit lyrics served only to make the whole hip-hop phenomenon more attractive to white youth. Thus, it appears that African American music forms are a viable model for communicating African American experience to a general audience as well as to the black community.

McMillan's opus constitutes a fictional blues autobiography in which she bears witness to the sanctifying power of love. Historically, the mass audience has not shown much interest in written accounts of black-on-black love, but generations of American audiences have identified their own experience with visions of love articulated by African American singers and songwriters. McMillan's decision to tell her stories in a blues romance mode is therefore a sound one. At the same time, given the firmly entrenched conventions of popular romance, narrating a blues romance in print requires a consummate degree of skill. Fortunately, McMillan is equal to the task.

BLUES ROMANCE

Black-on-black love in all forms is a central theme throughout McMillan's work. She continually counters stereotypes about African Americans that deny the existence of loving, supportive relationships within black families and black communities. In *Mama*, McMillan challenges stereotypes about the black family. In *Disappearing Acts*, she takes on an even more ambitious task, for if, as Henry Louis Gates, Jr., has asserted, the act of writing is inherently political/politicized for African Americans, then writing about loving relationships between black people must be even more so. If the ability to write proves that blacks have rational intellects, writing about black love simultaneously proves that blacks are capable of human feelings. Oddly enough, while Afro-Caribbean writers have long used the romance plot to develop allegorical visions of "the birth of a black nation," it was not until the late 1980s that African American women writers like McMillan began to assert that definitions of "the political" could encompass assertions of the power of love. In large measure, this oversight had to do with the expectations of the white audience that made up the bulk of every black writer's readership. The literary establishment often dismissed love stories as sentimental tripe. Meanwhile, African American writers needed to prove they could write serious fiction, and they had many seemingly more pressing issues to address.

African American romance also labors under built-in handicaps. The first is that the characters in a romance story must have enough auton- omy to commit themselves to each other. Political disenfranchisement, social segregation, and economic disempowerment made it difficult for African Americans to live out such commitments even after emancipa- tion. Great romantic tragedies arise from situations in which one or both of the principals lack this freedom, but most African American writers used these conditions to develop other modes of tragedy.

A second difficulty would-be authors of African American love stories have always faced is the mainstream audience's resistance to identifying with black men and women as romantic heroes and heroines. Depictions of sexual escapades in "Coontown" were a comic staple of the minstrel stage. This burlesque representation of black courtship and marriage has survived in American popular culture down to the present day—witness the crossover appeal of such African American sexually charged comedy films as *Boomerang* and *Strictly Business*, not to mention *Booty Call*. This tradition of burlesque has contributed to the feeling that romance is not a dignified subject for African American literature. Historically, even when African American writers did attempt to show that blacks can experience the "nobler sentiments," the story had to be couched in an elaborate narrative frame in order to make it acceptable to the main- stream audience. Nineteenth- and early-twentieth-century black women writers such as Pauline Hopkins, Frances E. W. Harper, Jesse Fauset, and Nella Larsen painted characters fair enough to pass for white before they endowed them with "tender feelings."

Problems of mimesis become especially acute in representations of black-on-black love. "Mimesis" refers to the degree of reality with which a work of art represents life. The double-consciousness dilemma imme- diately raises the question of whose "reality" will serve as the author's model: the reality of white publishers and readers, or the lived experi- ence shared by black writers and African American readers? Although mainstream popular romance offers the reader a chance to escape into an idealized reality, the author must still convince readers that the story is "true to life" in some way. This lifelike quality, also known as "veri- similitude," is more difficult to achieve when the protagonists are Afri- can American because, as noted above, a long history of oppression makes it more difficult for readers to suspend their disbelief in African American protagonists who are sufficiently empowered to serve as ro- mantic heroes and heroines.

If love is not possible within the parameters of everyday reality, it may be nurtured by supernatural forces. Indeed, subgenres of mainstream popular romance regularly feature angels, ghosts, vampires, and other supernatural creatures either directing the action or participating as one of the romantic leads. While love falls under the province of "secular" affairs, blues cosmology attributes a transformative, spiritual power to love experiences. Consequently, blues lyrics can proclaim the singer's willingness and ability to call on supernatural powers such as hoodooism or conjuring to win the object of desire's love.

Despite the potential for supernatural assistance in both popular romance and blues lyrics, African American popular romance eschews plots that depend on supernatural forces to bring about the happily-ever-after ending. This apparent anomaly would seem to indicate that African American audiences want the representation of black-on-black love to be as concrete as possible. Such insistence on verisimilitude may also indicate that black readers have different expectations about the function of popular romance than do mainstream readers. They may see African American romance as more than just an entertaining escape. Further, the absence of supernatural forces despite the strong tradition of conjuring in African American literary fiction suggests that African American romance writers have become comfortable in the knowledge that they are writing for an audience that does not need such inducements to believe in the possibility of black-on-black love.

McMillan therefore exhibited great prescience in shaping the plots of *Disappearing Acts* and *How Stella Got Her Groove Back*. Freed from the double-consciousness dilemma, she was able to manipulate conventions of form and manage audience expectations of verisimilitude in creative ways that enabled her to testify to her own truth. Consequently, her fiction has reached a mainstream readership as well as her core African American audience, effectively countering long-standing misrepresentations of black love in the process.

Representations of Black Love in American Popular Culture

The legacy of slavery complicates the representation of black love in mainstream forums. During slavery, slave marriages were not legally recognized. Slaves were required to obtain their masters' permission when choosing a mate. Some masters promoted love matches between the men and women on their plantations. Stable marriages conformed to masters' notions of Christian morality. Other masters believed that slaves with strong family bonds were less likely to run away and could be more easily cowed when threatened with the punishment of a loved one. Still other masters saw their slaves as breeding stock and bred couples together the way they might mate horses or cattle. Some objected when their slaves chose mates on other plantations, preferring that "natural increase" expand their own "stock" instead of that of their neighbors. At any time, slaveholders could sell one or both spouses to different masters, often separating loving couples for life. Masters also had the power to command a newly purchased slave to take a new mate, regardless of the individual's sense of commitment to a previous spouse.

One of the most pressing concerns former slaves brought to the Freedman's Bureau after the Civil War was assistance in locating spouses from whom they had been separated. The bureau also conducted mass weddings throughout the South for the hordes of couples who wanted to legalize their unions. As Herbert Gutman and other historians have demonstrated, African American families and communities were firmly bound together by warm ties of affection both in slavery and in freedom. Nevertheless, stereotypes that portray blacks as incapable of love persist even today. Slaveholders had propagated these myths as a rationalization for the practice of breaking up families on the auction block. Mark Twain exposes the absurdity of this attitude when he shows Huck Finn marveling over the realization that his friend Jim, the runaway slave, loved his wife and children: "I do believe he cared just as much for his people as white folks does for their'n. It don't seem natural, but I reckon it's so" (Twain 155).

Slavery also spawned many pernicious myths about black sexuality. Once again, masters rationalized their sexual abuse of slave women by portraying all black women as lascivious jezebels who seduced white men in order to satisfy their own inflamed passions. Stereotypes about black men held that their difficulties in fulfilling the male provider role were due to laziness, not an oppressive political and economic system. The only "manly" trait accorded black men in popular myth was sexual prowess. But here again, black male sexuality was portrayed as an unreasoning, animalistic lust that made them incapable of remaining faithful to a monogamous union.

In the face of these social myths, neither American literature nor American popular culture has yielded many stories about black men and women in love. The mass-culture industry has not often risked investing in representations of black love except perhaps as comic relief. The mass

audience would first have to be educated about African-American expectations of love in order to appreciate the porter's humble vision of
working together in harmony. Indeed, there are still many unanswered
questions about the function of romantic love in the lives of the slaves.
What made people risk loving when they knew that they were powerless
to protect their loved ones from being brutally punished or sold away?
How did couples define fidelity when neither black women nor black
men had the final say over their sexuality or reproductive capacity? How
did African American couples define masculinity, femininity, and the
relationship between the two gender roles when African American men
were deprived of all opportunities to wield the kind of power that defined white males as men and when African American women were
forced to labor at tasks that the dominant culture regarded as men's
work?

Representations of Black Love Within the Blues Aesthetic

Frustrated by the lack of documentation on the day-to-day existence
and inner life of African Americans during slavery, historian Lawrence
Levine borrowed heavily from the techniques of anthropologists and
folklorists to reconstruct "black culture and black consciousness" in his
1977 book by the same title. His method is a model for the practice of
African American Cultural Studies. In this influential work, Levine gives
special attention to studying African American music. By examining the
lyrics of the spirituals, work songs, and blues created by slaves and their
descendants, he is able to develop plausible hypotheses about social values in the black community from the time of slavery into the early twentieth century. In his chapter "The Rise of Secular Song," Levine notes
that there are distinct differences in the way that mainstream popular
songs and blues songs portrayed love from the 1920s through the 1940s.
Levine concludes that mainstream popular love songs created an idealistic vision of romantic love as a magical experience that simply happened, transfiguring all aspects of the lover's life as a result. Love
fulfilled childhood fantasies and dreams of heaven, but when love went
wrong, the lover was usually powerless to do much more than hope and
pray the situation would improve. In contrast, Levine finds that, although African Americans were certainly exposed to and influenced by
mainstream popular music, the blues allowed for a more realistic and

multifaceted vision of love. Blues songs were more explicit about physical intimacy, more frank about economic exchange as a component of
many relationships, more aware of the lover's flaws along with his or
her good points, and generally less sentimental. Brokenhearted lovers in
the blues were also more likely to assert self-confidence in their ability
to attract a more satisfactory mate.

Levine's work shows that black communities had developed forms for
representing romantic love, but these forms would not necessarily be
meaningful to a wider audience. McMillan's attempt to tell black love
stories to a general audience is therefore both artistically bold and politically significant because she draws primarily on the blues definition of
love rather than the romantic ideal traditionally favored by the mainstream American audience.

BLACK FEMINIST AESTHETICS IN AFRICAN
AMERICAN WOMEN'S FICTION

In her introduction to Carlene Hatcher Polite's torturous black love
story, *The Flagellants*, Claudia Tate comments on ways that black women
writers' aesthetic aims have deviated from the "historic limits of so-
called Negro fiction" since the mid-1960s. According to Tate, "Throughout virtually its entire history, Afro-American literature has argued for
the constitutional rights of black Americans" (Tate 1987, xxv). As a result,
the African American literary aesthetic has usually required that black
writers portray the struggles of black people in a social realist mode; that
black writers make petitions for racial equality central to their works,
whether they are writing fiction or nonfiction texts; and that black writers
create positive portrayals of black characters in order to counter pre-
vailing stereotypes about African Americans.

In contrast, Tate points out that black women writers such as Gayl
Jones, Toni Morrison, and Alice Walker "have been in the vanguard of
exploring personal liberty" rather than emphasizing civil liberty the way
that canonical male writers like Richard Wright, Ralph Ellison, and James
Baldwin had. As a result of their focus on personal rather than civil
liberty, Tate finds that contemporary black women writers tend not to
create idealized characters. They also tend not to address their works to
white readers in an effort to convince them that racism is wrong. Instead,
Tate argues that contemporary black women writers have created stories
that invite all readers to assume the roles of the central characters and

to participate in reflection on the nature and limits of personal freedom. While many of these writers have depicted extreme male brutality in their texts, Tate considers violent male characters like Jimson in *The Flagellants* or Mister in *The Color Purple* to be cautionary symbols of "the corruption of personal freedom." Although some critics have attacked these works for their negative depictions of black men, Tate points out that such critics "have disregarded the healing power of transformation that is central to these works" (Tate 1987, xxvii). Tate's remarks are as useful for situating Terry McMillan's work within a black female literary tradition as they are for illuminating Polite's earlier black-on-black love story. Many of the negative criticisms that have been leveled at McMillan's novels arise from the same clash of assumptions about the nature and function of African American writing that Tate describes.

Like Polite, Jones, Walker, Morrison, and a host of other twentieth-century black women writers, McMillan emphasizes the quest for personal liberty instead of championing civil liberty for the race as a whole. This does not mean that she glosses over the oppressive forces that curtail the freedoms of black people living in the United States. Rather, like her female peers, she is more interested in examining how individuals empower themselves and define their own sense of freedom. Moreover, because she is interested in questions of personal responsibility and choice, as are her female contemporaries, she creates characters who exhibit human flaws. Indeed, she allows one of her protagonists, Stella, to ironically dismiss her characters as "woe-is-me black women." Yet McMillan's heroines are almost all women of substance who reflect her generation's unprecedented success as professionals in the mainstream society. McMillan consistently challenges her characters to grow and attain greater levels of personal integration. Hence, her novels all celebrate "the healing power of transformation," which Tate sees as central to many twentieth-century black women's texts.

Spiritual Feminism

It is at this point that McMillan and her contemporaries rejoin the "spiritual feminism" that many nineteenth-century black women writers promoted in their texts. In her introduction to Emma D. Kelley-Hawkins's *Four Girls at Cottage City* (1898), Deborah E. McDowell explains that "one of the most popular arguments of the nineteenth century held that only the elevation of the spirit would obliterate racism and other 'earthly' injustices" (xxix). Thus, black women writers' concern with personal liberty (achieved in this case through spiritual redemption) is not wholly a recent development. McDowell describes Kelley-Hawkins as a precursor of "the spiritual feminism that is currently resonating throughout contemporary Afro-American women's fiction, as seen in such works as Ntozake Shange's *for colored girls who have considered suicide/when the rainbow is enuf* (1977), Toni Cade Bambara's *The Salt Eaters* (1980), and Alice Walker's *Meridian* (1976) and *The Color Purple* (1982)" (McDowell xxxvi). According to McDowell, "These contemporary black women writers see God as maternal, as a spiritual force within the female self, a force detached from the institutional, hierarchical, male-dominated church" (xxxvii). McMillan does not express these spiritual feminist values with the overt imagery employed by some of her contemporaries. Still, Mildred Peacock's quip "it ain't that I don't believe in God. I just don't trust his judgment" exemplifies a similar detachment from patriarchal Christianity. Further, Mildred as the "Mama" after which McMillan's first novel is named embodies the power of God as a maternal force, which resides within the female self. Indeed, Mildred has an abiding faith that women in their maternal role are like queen bees: they can do everything but fly.

Since McMillan's characters inhabit urban settings, they have little opportunity for communion with the forces of nature that frequently provide rich metaphors for spiritual transformation in the works of other black women writers. Mildred does experience an epiphany toward the end of *Mama*, but it occurs after she has run off the highway. Although she resorts to prayer at this moment, it is faith in herself rather than in God that enables her to change a flat tire for the first time in her life and extricate her car from the snowbank it has struck. The inert, snow-covered landscape along the interstate highway does not evoke spiritual presence in the way that Alice Walker's descriptions of rural Georgia or Zora Neale Hurston's earlier descriptions of rural Florida do. Even this outdoor scene is rare in McMillan's work since her characters, like those in both African American and mainstream women's fiction, most often move in interior, domestic spaces. Yet, McMillan's fictional worlds are not fully secularized. Instead, she has chosen a blues mode of representing spiritual experience rather than using more recognizable Christian iconography.

McDowell links Kelley-Hawkins's work to a larger nineteenth-century American women's tradition in which writers saw themselves as occupying a quasi-clerical status. She says that Kelley believed in the book as sermon and regarded her novels as "gospels in fictional form." She further compares Kelley to Charlotte Hood, a white writer who showed one of her characters being saved "by the experience of reading a woman's novel" (McDowell xxx). Once again, while McMillan rejects the Christian vision of redemption, her consistent use of the blues testimonial form casts her entire opus as a sermon in "a church for the fucking profane," which is how Vanessa characterizes her sister Stella's monologue in McMillan's most recent work.

McMillan's Personal Gospel

Audiences have in fact responded to McMillan's work and her public readings as secular sermons. "Camp meeting" is the term journalists have most often used to describe her public readings. This designation compares McMillan's ability to engage her audience in the traditional call-response exchange while moving them to a powerful catharsis with the skills of the traveling preachers who exhorted throngs in the tent revivals of the nineteenth century. African American journalist Isabel Wilkerson demonstrated similar recognition of McMillan's dissemination of her own personal gospel by entitling her 1996 article on McMillan's success "On Top of the Word." Wilkerson asserts that McMillan's novels "sit near the Bible on probably more nightstands than you know." She also categorizes *How Stella Got Her Groove Back* as McMillan's "latest sermon, which basically says that life is short, so do what makes you happy." Observing McMillan's "womanist street theory that seems to come off the top of her head but probably comes from the life and observations of her 44 years," Wilkerson concludes that McMillan "does not merely write books; she seems the sum total of them" (Wilkerson 51).

Thus, in Wilkerson's eyes, as in the eyes of her fans, McMillan's authority comes both from her art and from her life. Audiences embrace Terry McMillan's testimonials as they have embraced those of generations of blues divas because she offers insights into the possibility of personal transformation. As noted earlier, McMillan herself regards her novels as a record of her own spiritual growth; therefore, her works constitute a road map of "how I got ovuh." In the words of Zora Neale Hurston, "you've got to go there to know there." McMillan provides readers with signposts for the journey.

The "Conjure" Metaphor in Black Women's Fiction

Like many African American women writers who have emerged since the civil rights movement, McMillan claims Zora Neale Hurston as a literary ancestor. By anchoring the narrative frame of her works within black vernacular culture, Hurston began the process of translating the "secular" blues aesthetic into print. In her introduction to *Conjuring: Black Women, Fiction, and Literary Tradition*, Marjorie Pryse signals Hurston's importance as a model for how black women writers could assert the validity of their own worldview in an American literary tradition that had previously regarded authorship as a creative power derived from the Christian God. Thanks to her training in anthropology, Hurston was able to draw on African American folk magic to represent the creative power of black women, who, in the mainstream popular imagination, were not created in the image of God and presumably could not possess any artistic authority. According to Pryse, contemporary African American women writers share a special appreciation for Hurston's 1937 blues romance *Their Eyes Were Watching God* because "the black woman in Hurston's novel, finds her authority as storyteller both by her ability to 'conjure' up her past, and then to make storytelling itself serve as a connection between 'kissin'-friends' " (12–13). Pryse further emphasizes the importance of the contemporary black woman writer's relationship with her readers, for "the conjuring and the community of 'kissin'-friends' give her the power white men once said only comes from 'God' " (13). Pryse therefore uses "conjure" as a metaphor for the process by which African American women writers empower themselves as artists. As such, McMillan's adherence to the blues aesthetic places her in the company of her sister writers' communal elaboration of a spiritual feminism that rejects patriarchal Christianity.

McMillan nevertheless deviates from Hurston's conjuring legacy on several points. Tate would regard the figurative workings of Afro-centric folk magic in texts like *The Color Purple* as further evidence of contemporary black women writers' interest in advocating personal rather than civil liberty. Yet, while McMillan stresses the importance of personal liberty, she does not employ any magical or fantastical elements in her works. In *How Stella Got Her Groove Back*, the most idealized of her novels, Stella suggests to her confidante, Patrice, that Winston has worked some kind of obeah on her to win her love: "Don't they have like conjure women who work their mojos on you for a nominal fee?" she asks.

Mama
(1987)

The increased educational attainment and affluence of African Americans in the late twentieth century has produced a book-buying core audience for McMillan's work. Drawing on her own autobiographical experience, McMillan created in her first novel a story that many of these readers can identify with closely. McMillan's portrait of Mildred Peacock as the motivating force behind her children's upward mobility challenges pervasive stereotypes about black female-headed households by allowing readers to share her unique point of view. McMillan's debut novel consequently heralds her continuing interest in testifying about black women's power to define their own lives.

PLOT DEVELOPMENT

Terry McMillan's first novel tells the story of a working-class African American family living on the outskirts of Detroit in the 1960s and 1970s. The "Mama" of the story, Mildred Peacock, is a single mother with five children: Freda, Money, Bootsey, Angel, and Doll.

In Medias Res

Throughout *Mama*, McMillan demonstrates great skill at keeping readers interested in "what happens next." She achieves this goal by opening her story in medias res, in the middle of things. When the reader firsts meets Mildred Peacock, she is plotting to kill her husband, Crook, because he batters her. McMillan's strategy of starting in the middle of things immediately draws readers into Mildred's internal conflict—she does not want to kill Crook, she just wants to hurt him—and keeps readers turning pages to find out why she wants to hurt Crook and what she will eventually do. The opening chapter of *Mama* immerses Mildred in a variety of conflicts. McMillan pits her against her abusive husband. She illustrates Mildred's internal dilemma about whether to fight back or not and whether to leave Crook or not. Furthermore, by portraying the physical setting of one black woman's life outside Detroit in the turbulent 1960s, she alludes to the combined forces of racism and sexism that compound Mildred's predicament.

Mildred has always supplemented Crook's meager wages by doing domestic work, but once she divorces him, he ceases to contribute to the household finances, and it becomes more and more difficult for her to make ends meet. Thus, she alternates among domestic work, factory jobs, and welfare. She also seeks companionship and financial support from a series of different men. Increasingly, however, she relies on her oldest daughter, Freda, to help run the household. Indeed, when Mildred suffers a nervous breakdown, Freda is able to run things almost as well as her mother for the three weeks that Mildred is away recuperating.

Dual Protagonists

Traditionally, plots center on the goals and desires of a single main character struggling against the obstacles he or she must overcome to attain them. McMillan's novels consistently explore other techniques for structuring narrative. For example, *Mama* has two protagonists—Mildred and Freda. As she grows up, Freda observes Mildred's struggles against her husband, against poverty, and against her own shortcomings. Freda inherits her mother's struggles, then gradually confronts and overcomes them through the accumulation of wisdom and resources she has amassed from the combination of her mother's experience and her own.

After observing how hard her mother works, Freda vows to become rich and famous when she grows up so that she can take care of her mother. Mildred had always insisted that all her children would go to college. Freda fulfills this dream by moving to California and winning a scholarship to Stanford University. She remains close to her family while pursuing her career goals. Once she is established in California, she sends her mother a round-trip ticket and encourages her to move the whole family to Los Angeles. When Mildred agrees to the move, Freda finds an apartment for her mother and two of her younger sisters and helps them get settled in school or jobs. She has less success arranging Money's life because he is strung out on drugs.

In the meantime, Mildred's second daughter, Bootsey, remains in Michigan. She marries right after high school graduation and begins working at the Ford factory. By putting in many overtime shifts, she accumulates enough money to build and furnish her dream house. Slowly, however, Bootsey becomes disenchanted with these material goods and the lifestyle she has created for herself. Freda's career success also does not bring her the happiness she had imagined it would. After completing her bachelor of arts degree at Stanford, she enrolls in a master's program for journalism at New York University but feels shut out of the professional networks to which her white peers belong. She also has trouble getting her professors to take her articles on the African American community seriously, and she has even more trouble getting these pieces published.

Back in California, Mildred too is disillusioned with her life. As her youngest children Angel and Doll finish high school and become more independent, Mildred fears she is not needed anymore. Angel, the second to youngest daughter, marries a white man and seems to reject her upbringing and culture. Over the years, Mildred has accumulated an overwhelming burden of debt and finally gets arrested for writing bad checks. Mildred has also acquired a drinking problem and an addiction to her "nerve pills." Addiction affects her three oldest children as well. Her son, Money, spends several years in and out of jail because of his heroin addiction. Bootsey also becomes dependent on nerve pills under the strain of managing her household and working overtime to pay her bills. Freda, like her mother, becomes an alcoholic.

Despite their failings, McMillan presents her characters as whole human beings. Money kicks his heroin habit and becomes a strong family man with a steady job as an aeronautics technician. Bootsey decides to leave her husband and open her own business. In chapter 21, Freda turns thirty, while in the following chapter, Mildred faces her forty-eighth birthday. Passing these milestones motivates both mother and daughter to reassess their lives. In the process of redefining themselves, they prevail over many external and internal obstacles to achieve full self-actualization as autonomous African American women.

Central Conflict: My Mother/My Self

The central conflict in *Mama* might be described as a human-versus-self conflict. Human-versus-human conflicts with abusive romantic partners play a role in both protagonists' lives. Mildred's and Freda's struggles against racism and sexism also constitute an important human-versus-society conflict. Yet these challenges serve primarily to complicate Freda's and Mildred's efforts to define themselves as agents of their own destiny rather than as victims of oppressive circumstances. Further, one might argue that McMillan's dual protagonist technique constitutes a strong feminist statement about female identity formation within the primal relationship feminist author Nancy Friday has titled "my mother/my self." In her 1972 exploration of the bonds between mothers and daughters, Friday concluded that daughters unconsciously incorporate many facets of their mothers' identity. Thus, every woman's identity is a complex mixture of ways she is or is not like her mother. McMillan effectively captures the tension and enriching qualities of the mother/daughter identity crisis through skillful manipulation of narrative point of view.

NARRATIVE POINT OF VIEW

Strong conflict may capture readers' attention, but it is a narrator's perspective on circumstances and events that makes the action of a book believable and meaningful to readers. Narrators most commonly tell their stories either from an intimate, personal perspective, sharing their thoughts and feelings with readers, or from a more detached position that enables them to present other characters' motivations more objectively. These positions correspond roughly to first-person narration (i.e., "I saw") or third-person narration (i.e., "he saw"). Narrators may be more or less involved in the action of the story. A first-person central narrator is an active participant in events, while first-person peripheral narrators record their observations from a vantage point removed from the main action. A third-person narrator may have varying degrees of knowledge about the characters' motives. That is, the narrator may be more or less omniscient (all-knowing). The most omniscient narrators have a godlike ability to see any character's past, present, or future and to communicate judgments about the characters to the reader. Contemporary readers prefer to have some latitude in making their own judgments about the personalities they meet in books. Thus, authors of popular fiction usually limit the omniscience of their third-person narrators in some way.

At different points in the novel, McMillan's third-person narrator enters the minds of Mildred and each of her children, recording events from their distinct points of view. However, while the narrative follows one character's impressions, readers are completely immersed in that character's point of view and are not permitted to know anything that the character could not observe. This type of limited omniscience is called "third-person shifting narration." In *Mama*, the narrative point of view shifts most often between Mildred and Freda. Hence, they are the main viewpoint characters in the story. By alternately presenting Mildred's and Freda's point of view, McMillan invites readers to share their experiences. The third-person shifting narration encourages readers to imagine how they would feel in the same situation and what they would do. Since most readers of contemporary popular fiction are seeking opportunities to participate in an emotional experience, contemporary popular fiction emphasizes character development over plot, and a skilled writer like McMillan wins fans because she has mastered techniques of characterization that make readers embrace her characters as believable and likeable human beings.

CHARACTER DEVELOPMENT

There are two main approaches to characterization: authorial presentation and direct character presentation. The first strategy works well when an author needs to convey information about a character in a short space. For example, in chapter 2 of *Mama*, the narrator describes the Red Shingle bar and its owner, Fletcher Armstrong: "Fletcher had green eyes and peach skin. He didn't associate with the regular black people of Point Haven because he thought he was better than they were" (25). Here the narrator informs readers that Fletcher is conceited because he has light skin. Since he is a minor character, allowing readers to discover this attitude for themselves by observing him in various scenes would slow down the plot. Authorial presentation is therefore an efficient way of letting readers know what minor characters are like. Still, most readers prefer to formulate their own opinions about the main characters in a story. The techniques of direct character presentation cater to this preference by allowing readers to observe characters' appearances, actions, speech, and thoughts for themselves.

McMillan shows her flair for dialogue as a technique of direct characterization in the opening of chapter 2. " 'Kill him,' slurred Curly Mae, as she fell back in the recliner on Mildred's sun porch." With these two uttered words, McMillan shows readers that Mildred's sister-in-law is a loyal friend. The husband she is advising Mildred to kill is her own brother. Her advice also suggests that, despite her loyalty, her approach to life is not very pragmatic. Her actions indicate that she is drunk, and they also enable the reader to envision the setting in which the scene takes place. Yet McMillan does not tell readers, "Curly Mae got drunk and told Mildred to kill her husband." Instead, she lets them witness the scene directly. Allowing readers to discover for themselves what a character looks like, thinks, does, and says provides them with a more satisfying illusion of encountering full human beings.

McMillan draws on the full range of characterization techniques to gradually introduce readers to Freda over the course of the first chapter. We first hear of Freda when Mildred is musing on the trouble her eldest daughter's appearance has caused with her husband. Mildred reviews in her thoughts how Crook had always disliked her friend Percy because it was rumored that Freda was really Percy's daughter. The fact that both men have light skin, wavy hair, and high cheekbones makes it equally probable that either of them could have been Freda's father since these are also distinguishing features of her appearance.

Next we hear and see Freda attempting to comfort her sisters while their parents enact a ritual scene of domestic violence: " 'Why they try to kill each other, then do the nasty?' Bootsey asked Freda. 'Mama don't like doing it,' Freda explained. 'She only doing it so Daddy won't hit her no more' " (11). Freda's diction reveals her youth as well as her class and ethnic background. Without any other clues readers might guess that Freda is a young African American girl here because the double-negative construction "won't hit her no more" is a common feature of vernacular black English. To "do the nasty" is also an African American slang term for sexual intercourse. Not all African Americans use these dialect forms, and the double negative is used by many working-class speakers of various ethnic backgrounds; however, Freda's speech makes it unlikely that she is a member of a well-educated, middle-class family. This brief exchange also illustrates her maternal concern for her younger siblings and demonstrates that mothering is already a strong facet of her identity.

As noted, the third-person shifting narration McMillan uses in *Mama* gives readers access to the thoughts of each member of the Peacock brood. This technique allows readers to see the strengths and weaknesses of the other four children in the family even though Mildred and Freda are the main viewpoint characters. For example, Money is the next oldest after Freda. The only male in a house full of women, he somehow learns to fix everything that breaks around the house, despite the fact that he does not have a male mentor to initiate him into the manly art. As a young man, however, his mechanical genius is overshadowed by heroin addiction. McMillan reveals all this information about the character through her skillful use of narrative techniques.

Bootsey, the next oldest girl, is in no way short of strength. Like Mildred and Freda, she is determined to realize her goals. She focuses on obtaining economic security and willingly works years of overtime at her factory job in order to build a fine house and fill it with material goods. Bootsey is the only one of Mildred's children to disregard her mother's insistence on the value of education. In contrast, Angel, like Freda, excels academically. She obtains a master's degree and becomes an English teacher, but her yearning for assimilation into mainstream middle-class society is so great that she marries outside her race and turns her back on her own culture. Doll, the youngest child, is less concerned with acquiring the trappings of wealth or respectability. She shares Mildred's freewheeling attitude toward sexuality and becomes pregnant in her teens. Unsure who the father of her child is, she remains at home for a time and abdicates her maternal responsibilities to Mildred. Eventually, however, she exhibits her mother's fierce independence by moving out and establishing her own home. Motherhood means everything to Mildred, and she regards her children as her future. McMillan's skillful use of characterization techniques effectively engages readers in Mildred's rich but unconventional family life.

CULTURAL CONTEXT

Transformations in the Social Status of African Americans

Mama reflects many transformations in the social status of African Americans. Mildred's family is among the millions of blacks who left the South between World War I and World War II in search of more equal opportunities. This mass movement is known as the "Great Migration," and it swelled the African American population of industrial centers around northern cities like Detroit to as much as 40 percent of the total metropolitan population, despite the fact that African Americans constituted only about 11 percent of the U.S. population. In fact, between 1960 and 1970, the time period that corresponds with Freda's childhood, the black population of Detroit increased from 28 percent to 43 percent of the total. While this increase might partially have been due to continued in-migration of rural blacks, it was probably also influenced by out-migration of whites moving to the suburbs. The existence of prejudice that often motivated such "white flight" is one reason the North did not turn out to be the Promised Land.

At the end of chapter 3, McMillan describes residential segregation in the various towns around Point Haven, Michigan, where Mildred lives with her children. She paints a landscape in which the prospects for social mobility are bleak. Half the literate population does factory work while less well-educated men work for the Department of Sanitation. Women like Mildred who never finished high school do domestic work or depend on welfare, but Mildred has higher aspirations for her children, determined to do whatever she needs to so they can all go to college. Thus, she espouses the traditional African American faith in education as the key to greater freedom within American society.

In their own ways, in their own good time, Mildred's children eventually do realize her dream and secure a foothold in the middle class. Their tenuous upward mobility reflects the experience of many African Americans born during the post–World War II baby boom. Mildred insists that her children finish high school. Armed with these diplomas, Freda, Doll, and Angel can work their way through college while attending tax-supported state schools. All across the country during this period, minorities and women were matriculating at colleges and universities in unprecedented numbers. Between 1965 and 1985, African

American college enrollment increased from 274,000 to 1,742,000 (U.S. Bureau of the Census, 1988 140). Women of all races and ethnic groups earned almost twice as many college degrees in 1984 than in 1966. Many of McMillan's readers, therefore, can identify with Mildred's children because they or members of their family have followed the same path.

Mildred's son, Money, is initially less successful than his sisters, but after securing a job in an aeronautics manufacturing plant, he too is able to complete his education and provide a secure economic base for his family. Thus, McMillan's first novel reflects the unprecedented social mobility that was available to African Americans in the 1960s and 1970s. Indeed, the increased educational attainment and affluence of African Americans has provided a core audience for McMillan's work without which her success in reaching a mass audience would not have been possible. The relationship between literacy and increased freedom is therefore not only crucial for Mildred's children to realize her dreams for them, it is also a key component of McMillan's own status as the first best-selling African American popular fiction writer.

Mama and the Black Matriarchy Theory

Mama not only reflects transformations in the social status of African Americans, it also reflects transformations in women's roles in society. More specifically, McMillan uses the novel to expose some "home truths" about black women's experiences to a mass audience. First published in 1987, McMillan's debut novel appeared at a time when black feminist scholars were diligently researching and writing about black female experience. In great measure, they were motivated by the desire to deconstruct old stereotypes about black women. One of the most politically charged of these stereotypes was the myth of the single black mother as a domineering matriarch. Elements of this stereotype date back to slavery days, but the "black matriarchy" theory as an explanation for all the social ills that kept blacks in poverty was crystallized in "The Negro Family: The Case for National Action," a report commissioned by Senator Daniel Patrick Moynihan and published in 1965.

In 1964 and 1965, Congress passed legislation shoring up constitutional guarantees of "equal justice under the law." Known as the Civil Rights Act of 1964 and the Voting Rights Act of 1965, these laws were designed to guarantee equal access to public educational institutions and equal accommodation in public venues, such as restaurants, hotels, theaters, and public conveyances, as well as to protect the voting rights of all U.S. citizens. Senator Moynihan was sympathetic to the civil rights movement, but since he was from New York, he saw that the problems of his black constituents required more than just cosmetic desegregation. His report concluded that the problems of the urban black poor stemmed primarily from the structure of their families, of which 25 percent were headed by single women. Moynihan argued that a family pattern in which women headed households reversed the social norm and therefore prevented children raised in such households from successfully adapting to and competing within the larger society.

African Americans objected strenuously to Moynihan's characterization of the Negro family as "a tangle of pathology." Black scholars like Herbert Gutman, author of *The Black Family in Slavery and Freedom*, set out to prove that Moynihan had wrongly portrayed black families as matriarchal and unstable. Still, many African Americans accepted the idea that "restoring" black men to a position of dominance within their families and communities was essential for continued racial uplift. As a result, many African American women who were active in the civil rights movement remained in the background and allowed male leaders to take the spotlight. Further, while African American women were aware of the nascent feminist movement, many felt that loyalty to the men of their race took precedence over the struggle for gender equality. Such women regarded sexism as a private matter to be resolved within the black community or as a secondary issue that could be addressed only after racist oppression had been overthrown.

By the time McMillan published *Mama* in 1987, female-headed households constituted at least 42 percent of all African American families (Taeuber 288). More than 56 percent of all African American children were born out of wedlock, and 36 percent of all African American children under age eighteen were living in poverty (Taeuber 38, 199). Low educational attainment and juvenile delinquency, two of the markers of pathology that Moynihan had catalogued, had also increased in severity. African American leaders began to sound the alarm and call for African American communities to take responsibility for building stable, two-parent families. Meanwhile, the Republican administrations of Ronald Reagan and George Bush actively sought to dismantle most of the social service programs that had been established twenty years earlier under President Lyndon Johnson's "War on Poverty." Out of this political climate arose a new stereotype of the black "welfare queen," who allegedly produced a string of illegitimate children by different fathers in order to collect additional welfare benefits.

The primary function of popular fiction is to entertain the audience. But to write a novel in the late 1980s from the perspective of a single black mother was also to take a strong political position. At the beginning of the story, we see Mildred Peacock as a battered wife, but McMillan does not portray her as a victim. Through three husbands and affairs with "unsuitable" partners such as married, younger, and white men, through occasional prostitution and an arrest for writing bad checks, McMillan humanizes a character who might only have reinforced the worst stereotypes about black matriarchs by allowing readers to share her point of view. Mildred exemplifies everything mainstream society says a mother should not be, and yet, not only does she define herself first and foremost as a mother, but her children's success vindicates her unconventional style of mothering. Mildred Peacock, then, in her fictional existence, suggests that black female-headed households might not be the unredeemable "tangle of pathology" they were commonly supposed to be.

THEMATIC ISSUES

Motherhood

McMillan uses her craft to make Mildred Peacock a powerful character whose story engages readers in a full-bodied emotional experience. At the same time, she develops the theme of motherhood throughout the novel as a means of commenting on the parameters of female identity in general and black female identity in particular.

First and foremost, Mildred regards motherhood as power. On the second page of *Mama*, McMillan's narrator reveals the gossip about Freda's paternity. Paternity is therefore uncertain, but motherhood is a solid basis of power—perhaps the only kind of power an uneducated black woman could aspire to in Midred's time and place. Early on, McMillan shows Mildred exercising her maternal power as she orders her children around. In resolving to leave her husband, Mildred asserts, "These ain't your damn kids. They mine" (15). She sees the children as an extension of herself: "When she pulled the brush back and up through their thick clods of nappy hair, she smiled because it was her own hair she was brushing" (16). Thus, the children represent Mildred's future.

During the course of the novel, however, Mildred is forced to question and redefine motherhood as the foundation of her identity. As her children grow up and leave home, her power diminishes. The body that had allowed her to produce these miracles also withers with age. Once her children are adults, Mildred has a hard time envisioning a future for herself. For a time, she tries to make caring for her elderly father replace caring for her children, but when he dies, she is cast adrift.

Though motherhood empowers, it also demands tremendous self-sacrifice. Over the years, Mildred does many things to provide for her children that gradually erode her sense of self-worth. Self-sacrifice therefore contributes to her alcohol and drug addiction. Finally, she begins to resent what she sees as her children's ingratitude. She lashes out against them in hurtful ways. By presenting the evolution of Mildred's character, McMillan shows both the benefits and frustrations women experience in defining themselves as mothers.

Mildred's Philosophy of Child Rearing

McMillan presents Mildred's unconventional but successful philosophy of child rearing to demonstrate that black female-headed families are not pathological. In particular, Mildred makes three vows to her children that constitute the core principles of their upbringing. She vows they will always eat, they will not look like orphans, and they will go to college. Upholding her promise that her children will always be fed forces Mildred to make many painful sacrifices. She works demeaning jobs; at times, she trades her self-respect for some economic assistance. Applying for welfare is one such blow to her pride. On another occasion, she engages in casual prostitution. She even enters into a marriage of convenience in an effort to secure a more stable financial base for her children.

Mildred's second promise—"You won't look like orphans"—becomes the basis of her own and her children's self-respect and self-esteem. She insists that all five of her kids always have decent clothes to wear. She is careful to replace clothes that they outgrow or wear out. She also insists that they keep themselves, their clothes, and whatever house they are living in spotlessly clean. To Mildred, cleanliness is the foundation of decency and self-respect. This aspect of her character actively belies the stereotype of the welfare mother as lazy and slovenly.

At the same time, Mildred's obsession with external appearances leads her to enmesh herself in a web of falsehoods. She manipulates the welfare system, avoids paying taxes, defrauds creditors, and writes bad checks in her effort to provide the trappings of decency for her family. McMillan shows the human motive behind these "immoral" actions: Mildred wants to provide for her children in a system that denies her the means to do so. Neither welfare nor jobs she is qualified for pay enough for her to keep her children from "looking like orphans." Meanwhile, McMillan clearly shows what Mildred's pattern of lies costs her in personal terms—she experiences a very painful alienation from her own desires and goals. Freda learns to lie from her mother, and living in denial ultimately costs her even more than it costs Mildred. Her denial prevents her from establishing fulfilling intimate relationships and achieving her professional goals. Part of the identity formation process in the novel is for both mother and daughter to face the truth about themselves and each other.

Mildred is most insistent on the value of education, although she herself is barely literate. The key to her children's success is that they take this message to heart. At the end of the novel, Mildred finally decides to apply this advice to herself. At last, she is able to envision a future for herself. She decides to seek certification to run a day-care center. Thus, she returns to her original belief that motherhood or nurturing is empowering.

Mildred makes mothering an end in itself, but she sums up her definition of the good life in the word "decency." By this, she means having a good husband, healthy children, and peace of mind. Mildred is never able to realize this ideal. She has healthy children but no husband (most of the time) and very little peace of mind. Bootsey tries hardest to realize her mother's vision of the good life. She forgoes college and right after high school marries an older man who seems like solid husband material. She works long hours in the automobile factory to acquire the kind of financial security Mildred was never able to provide. She has a large custom-built house and fills it with all the trappings of consumer culture. Yet, around the time that Freda and Mildred begin to emerge from denial, Bootsey also realizes that she is not happy with this dream and leaves her husband. Bootsey's awakening illustrates that Mildred's vision of decency does not suit the reality of her own or her daughters' lives and that they must all let go of this unattainable ideal in order to fully actualize themselves.

The most unconventional aspect of Mildred's mothering is her frankness about her sexuality: " 'These is *my* kids,' she would say, 'and this ain't half the shit they gon' see in this world, so they might as well find out from me now before some ignorant ass in the streets gives it to 'em wrong' " (110). Mildred chooses to divorce rather than kill her abusive husband. As a result, she must decide early on how to balance her sexual life with her role as a mother. When she finds a steady boyfriend, she rejects the notion that mothers should deny their sexual needs and opts instead to tell her children about him and conduct the affair in the open.

After this relationship ends, Mildred takes up with a married man. Despite her earlier scruples, she justifies the relationship to her children, asserting that Spooky Cooper *used* to be Miss Francis's husband, but now he makes her feel better than her children's father ever did. During this interlude, McMillan shows that a woman's passion can make her momentarily forget her maternal identity: "She couldn't remember her children, by name or by face, and in her heart, she didn't even have any" (79–80). Of course, Mildred soon reaps what she had sown by indulging in this affair. Spooky goes back to his wife. Mildred then agrees to marry an unattractive older man named Rufus. Explaining the decision to her children, she says, "He can help me pay these bills" (88) and asserts that she is too old to marry for love.

Rufus, like Crook, becomes abusive, so Mildred swiftly divorces him. She picks up the financial slack by meeting a white "john" across the border in Canada every Sunday for three months. She does not, however, reveal this relationship to her children. Indeed, part of her justification for breaking it off is that she is tired of lying to them about where she goes. Later, in her children's teen years, Mildred does introduce them to a white boyfriend named Big Jim. Their initial objections to his race are overcome by the fact that he has ready cash, which is something that Mildred's other boyfriends had never had.

Of all her escapades, it is Mildred's relationship with a younger man that most thoroughly scandalizes her children. After her second divorce, Mildred rents an extra room to a young man named Billy Callahan. Soon they become lovers, although Billy is twelve years younger than his thirty-something landlady. One night Freda discovers them in bed together. She is shocked and calls Mildred a whore. Mildred, true to form, refuses to apologize for gratifying her physical needs. Instead, she berates Freda for being nosey enough to check up on her. After her mother explains that women sometimes need male companionship, Freda accepts the relationship and, in turn, explains their mother's "needs" to her siblings.

Mother/Daughter Rivalry

Significantly, McMillan chooses to pick up Mildred's story just when her daughter Freda is approaching puberty. Psychologists often regard a girl's adolescent years as a period of sexual rivalry with her mother. In the teen years, girls discover the power of their developing sexuality, while mothers who feel insecure about the waning of their own sexual attractiveness may feel threatened. Adolescence is also the period in which children struggle to establish an identity that is distinct from their parents. Moreover, for many women of Freda's generation, the greater sexual freedom and increased career opportunities open to women intensified the desire to define an identity distinct from that of their mothers. Many young women of Freda's generation rejected motherhood outright as the foundation of female identity. Demographers projected that 90 percent of women born between 1946 and 1964 would eventually become mothers, but this increasingly educated group of women has created a significant trend in delaying motherhood until they have completed their educational goals and have established a foothold in the career of their choice. The average age of first pregnancy has risen two years since the mid-1950s, from just over twenty to just under twenty-three (McLaughlin et al. 123).

Given this demographic context, the central dilemma of a novel entitled *Mama* could easily have been the human-versus-human conflict between mother and daughter as the daughter struggles to create a new kind of female identity. In contrast, when Mildred leaves Freda in charge of the household, Freda discovers that she enjoys the power of the "little mother" role. On the surface, Freda defines a life for herself that is very different from her mother's. Mildred defines herself through her biological function; having babies makes her life meaningful. Freda defines herself through intellectual creation. Of all Mildred's children, she is the only one who does not marry, the only one who does not bear children, and the only one who has an abortion. Mildred is a high school dropout, while Freda completes college and works on a graduate degree.

Nevertheless, all the choices that differentiate Freda from her mother are motivated by her desire to "mother" her mother. As a young girl,

Freda begins to define herself by emulating the only model of an independent woman in her life—her mother. She becomes proficient in all the domestic tasks associated with running a household, and she dominates her younger siblings just as Mildred dominates them all: "Freda loved the power she had playing mama" (84). At the same time, it is Freda's desire to mother her mother that leads her to reject motherhood as the sum total of her identity. Instead, she vows to make something of herself so that her mother will no longer have to scrub floors. In the final analysis, caretaking is just as much the foundation of Freda's identity as it is the bedrock of her mother's self-image.

In the late 1980s, when *Mama* first appeared, professional women recognized, as the saying goes, that they had become the men they wanted to marry. Freda becomes a white-collar wage earner not to usurp male privilege, but to extend the nurturing power she saw her mother exercising when she was growing up. Mildred compared women in their maternal role to queen bees—they could do everything but fly. Freda learns to use this nurturing power as a means of self-actualization and empowerment outside the parent-child relationship. Ultimately, Freda's example inspires Mildred to redefine the meaning and function of her own nurturing power. Over the course of the novel, Mildred and Freda learn how to better nurture each other by nurturing themselves.

Nurturing and Self-Definition

In this process of self-definition depicted throughout *Mama*, Freda and Mildred also redefine their own relationship. Soon after divorcing her first husband, Mildred faces the difficult task of providing Christmas presents for her children on an extremely tight budget. She decides to ask Freda, the oldest, to wait for her presents until the following month. Both Freda and Mildred fall back on stoic strength at this moment. They are unable to embrace, unable to comfort each other or themselves.

Subsequently, Freda continues to help Mildred shoulder the burden of mothering. She even manages the household for several weeks when Mildred succumbs to a nervous breakdown. Freda makes herself almost indispensable, and yet both she and her mother are able to accept the inevitability of her growing up and moving out on her own. Once Freda is settled in California, her relationship with Mildred begins to evolve. Mildred comes to recognize Freda as a friend as well as a daughter.

McMillan develops a ritual exchange between Freda and Mildred to symbolize their relationship. Whenever they get together after periodic separations, Freda gives her mother gifts like earrings and brassieres. Both mother and daughter maintain the fiction that these are items Freda had bought for herself. This premise indicates that mother and daughter are mirror images of each other. They are the same size and share the same taste in the most personal and intimate markers of femininity. Mildred "finds" the earrings and bras by snooping through Freda's luggage or dresser drawers. Rather than bristling at this invasion of her privacy, Freda always maintains, "I put them there for you to find." Thus, her intimacy with Mildred assumes that her mother should have access to the most private compartments of her life. Mildred usually asks to "borrow" these items after she has found them, but they both know that Freda will not ask her mother to return them.

Through this ritual, McMillan develops a powerful representation of female identity. Earrings are a socially constructed sign of femininity. Women are not born with earrings. They learn to wear them as part of their socialization. Girls are not born with breasts either, and wearing brassieres is also a social convention. Yet the brassiere signifies the biological aspects of womanhood. When a girl has developed enough to begin wearing bras, she is physically en route to becoming a woman.

McMillan uses breast imagery to signify women's nurturing power throughout the novel. Mildred frequently observes and reflects on her breasts as symbols. When they begin to wither and sag with age, they remind her that her mothering days are over, causing her to feel disempowered. Similarly, when Mildred asks Freda to wait on her Christmas presents, McMillan notes, "although her chest was filling up with air and her training bra was rising and falling as if she had breasts, Freda was trying hard to be as strong as Mildred" (45). Here the brassiere/breast imagery shows that self-sacrifice is part of Freda's training in becoming a woman.

In fact, the other element of Mildred and Freda's ritual exchange symbolizes the pain mother and daughter have to inflict on each other in the process that molds the girl into a socially acceptable image of woman. Mildred always asks Freda to pluck her eyebrows for her. When Freda finishes, she regards her mother's face as something she has created. Through this role reversal, McMillan makes an important comment on female identity formation. On the one hand, she shows how all daughters create an image of their mothers and use that image to define themselves. On the other hand, the ritual exchange illustrates Freda's mothering of her mother. She covets the power her mother had over her as a child. By creating her mother, she assumes some of this power. Meanwhile, Freda's very existence ratifies Mildred's femininity. In conceiving and giving birth to her first child, Mildred created herself as a woman and as a mother. Before Freda was born, Mildred was neither a mother nor a biologically complete woman. Freda's birth has therefore established a powerful female identity for Mildred. Consequently, Freda is as much the author of Mildred's maternal identity as Mildred is the author of Freda's existence.

The unusual dual protagonist structure of the novel reflects the permeable "my mother/my self" identity that Mildred and Freda create, not through head-on, human-versus-human conflict, but through exploration of the self, both internally and in relation to (m)other. By the end of the novel, Mildred and Freda have learned to nurture the self and are therefore able to nurture each other. For the first time they are able to embrace:

> Mildred's breasts felt full against her own, and Freda couldn't tell whose were whose. They held each other up. They patted each other's back as if each had fallen and scraped a knee and had no one else to turn to for comfort. It seemed as if they hugged each other for the past and for the future. (307)

In *Mama*, McMillan uses the theme of motherhood to present female identity as a both/and relational experience rather than an either/or, me/not me oppositional experience. It is therefore appropriate to apply feminist psychoanalytic critical theory to further examine the mother/daughter dynamic in the novel.

ALTERNATIVE INTERPRETATION: PSYCHOANALYTIC CRITICISM

Psychoanalytic literary criticism derives from the theories of Sigmund Freud, Carl Jung, Alfred Adler, and their disciples. At the turn of the century, these psychoanalysts believed they were conducting scientific inquiry into the workings of the human mind. Thus, they regarded psychoanalysis as a science as well as an art. In order to be accepted as truth, a scientific theory should be universally applicable. Once psychoanalysis gained the status of scientific truth, people who grew up in families like Freda's, which did not match the expected "norm," were suspected of harboring neuroses and other kinds of psychological mal-adjustments. This kind of ethnocentric thinking enabled the Moynihan report to gain wide credibility as an explanation for why so many African Americans found themselves trapped in a cycle of poverty. McMillan's debut novel resists traditional psychoanalytic interpretation, but this approach effectively illustrates how *Mama* challenges stereotypes about black female-headed households through its representation of a working class black family achieving the American Dream.

Freud pioneered the concept of the unconscious mind as the repository of impulses which the waking consciousness is not aware of. In order to explore how these repressed impulses affected behavior, Freud encouraged his patients to "free-associate," that is to speak freely whatever thoughts came to mind. He would then search for symbolic meaning in what they said. Examining symbolism in narrative was a technique familiar to literary critics; therefore, Freud's system for interpreting symbols was a very attractive tool to some. Indeed, Freud drew the Oedipus complex, another one of his most influential concepts, from classical Greek literature. In the Oedipus myth, a young man named Oedipus who has been raised by foster parents inadvertently kills his biological father and marries his biological mother. Freud used the Oedipus myth to describe his observation that male children harbored the unconscious desire to have their mother's affection all to themselves. He believed that in order to become psychologically healthy adults, boys had to resolve this oedipal drama by transferring their affection for the mother to an adult female sexual partner. This process was complicated by the fact that the boy's closest model of masculinity, his father, was also his greatest rival.

For decades Freud's theories held wide currency both in the medical profession and in the humanities. From the beginning, however, the Oedipus complex did not explain women's experiences as well as it seemed to explain men's. In Freud's time, women were almost exclusively the primary caregivers for small children. Not surprisingly, psychoanalysts asserted that the first love object for all children was the mother. The great mystery was, if children did feel libidinous urges towards the female caregiver, why then would girls ever transfer their desire to men? Yet in the popular understanding of psychoanalysis, women who rejected marriage and motherhood as their biological destiny were diagnosed as having failed to resolve their Oedipus complex and as suffering from neurotic penis envy as a result.

Early women psychoanalysts like Karen Horney and Melanie Klein asserted that female gender identity was socially constructed rather than biologically determined. They pointed out that the society in which they lived was male-dominated and that if girls and women did envy men, it was for the social power that having a penis represented. In the late 1960s and early 1970s, feminist scholars like Juliet Mitchell and other theorists began a rigorous re-evaluation of psychoanalysis in part because it provided one of the first theories of how people form gender identity. In the 1950s, American mass media had also popularized an interpretation of psychoanalysis which tended to trace all developmental difficulties back to the child's relationship with the mother. This "blame the mother" attitude infuriated many women and led feminists like Nancy Friday, author of *My Mother/Myself*, to explore mother/daughter relationships in more intimate detail than ever before.

Today various studies indicate that the number of women who have been sexually abused as children might be as high as one in three. Thus, it has become apparent that Freud's gender bias prevented him from fully comprehending female experience. Meanwhile, Marxist or materialist critics have added other pertinent arguments to the reexamination of psychoanalysis. The first is that psychoanalytic theory derives primarily from clinical observation of the upper-middle-class people who could afford psychoanalytic treatment. The theory might therefore not be valid for explaining working-class mores and identity, which are more likely to be affected by economic deprivations than by real or perceived deficiencies in parental affection. The second is that capitalist society as a whole is subject to the kind of examination psychoanalysts have applied to individuals. Scholars like Herbert Marcuse have asserted that studying mass psychology in this way might make psychoanalysis a useful tool for understanding why the oppressed continue to accept the inequalities of the capitalist system. It might also provide a tool for transforming consciousness and motivating the masses to revolt.

Given the choices available to her within her socioeconomic context, Mildred's serial marriages and casual experiences with prostitution, as well as her drug and alcohol addiction, are survival strategies rather than moral flaws or manifestations of an unresolved Oedipus complex. McMillan gives even more weight to socioeconomic realities in her next novel, *Disappearing Acts*.

him and that there is some hope for them to have a future
f he can get his "constitution" together before too long.
e plot McMillan chose for her second novel reflects her pio-
novative spirit. As she did in *Mama*, McMillan uses dual pro-
stead of organizing her plot around the obstacles that stand
e character and his or her goals. Once again, instead of pitting
characters against each other, her story explores the internal,
sus-self conflicts each one faces. Zora and Franklin must learn
mselves before they can risk trusting each other completely.
hey both grow over the course of the novel, they do not arrive
t of full confidence in each other before the novel ends. Mc-
s not provide the happy ending that is essential to the popular
enre, but her ending does not preclude a positive outcome.

IVE POINT OF VIEW

n's most obvious departure from the conventions of popular
s perhaps her first-person alternating narration. Popular ro-
ost exclusively employs third-person limited omniscient nar-
e heroine is typically the main viewpoint character, but by the
this convention was beginning to change. Romance readers
rs found that incorporating at least some of the hero's percep-
the story made it more satisfying. McMillan, however, estab-
olute parity between her hero and heroine. The point of view
een Franklin and Zora in each chapter. Male and female read-
ppreciated this intimate insight into the dynamics of the re-
, and when the book appeared, McMillan received specific
her understanding of the male psyche.
who have condemned McMillan as a "male basher" since the
al success of *Waiting to Exhale* would do well to reread *Dis-
Acts*. Reviewing his experience with black women, Franklin
s, "One chick, I liked her a lot. Her name was Theresa, and she
hen you called her Terri" (2). Enumerating her sterling qual-
klin remembers that she worked at a bank, was a good cook,
ts, and "knew a call when she heard one too" (3). By inserting
name into Franklin's relationship history, McMillan suggests
lin is a man she has known and loved, a man whom she can
ave his say about a woman like herself without becoming bitter
ve. This intimate dialogue between the sexes is uncommon in

4

Disappearing Acts
(1989)

The historical experience of African American men in the United States
has challenged them to forge a new definition of manhood—one that
cannot rest solely on providing material comfort for the family. McMillan's second novel features a skillful characterization of an African American man struggling to meet this challenge. By alternating the first-person
narration between this man and the woman who loves him, McMillan
makes effective use of a love story to lodge a serious social protest. At
the same time, she builds on romance and blues romance traditions to
provide a popular base that she balances with a black feminist vision of
the nature and function of art.

PLOT DEVELOPMENT

Disappearing Acts bravely and realistically depicts love between African
Americans in ways that were formerly impossible. When twenty-nine-
year-old Zora Banks goes hunting for a new apartment in Brooklyn, she
meets tall, dark, and handsome Franklin Swift, who is renovating the
unit. The attraction between the two is so strong that just a few days
after Zora rents the apartment, Franklin spends the night with her. However, Zora's friends are skeptical about the new man in her life. She is a
college graduate who teaches music in a junior high school. Franklin is

a high school dropout who does construction work—when he can find a job. What Zora and Franklin share are their dreams of artistic fulfillment. Franklin is a skilled artisan who makes handcrafted furniture. Zora is a singer/songwriter saving her money to produce a demo tape and audition for recording contracts. Thus, the real difficulty in the romance is not that their backgrounds are so different. Rather, Franklin and Zora struggle to work together as a couple without losing sight of their own individual goals and identities.

Despite many years of experience, discriminatory hiring practices have kept Franklin from breaking into the trade unions that can make construction work a stable career. Yet construction is the only well-paid work he is qualified to do. Franklin had sworn not to get involved with any women until he had figured out how to get his "constitution" together, but he finds Zora irresistible. In the early days of their relationship, she seems like a woman who can help him make the kinds of positive changes he has been wanting to make in his life. Through an organization called "A Dream Deferred," which seeks to get minority workers into the trade unions, Franklin lands a good construction job soon after he and Zora begin seeing each other. He uses his first paycheck to help Zora get her piano out of storage and is enchanted when she sings for him.

Disappearing Acts, however, is not a fairy-tale romance. Franklin is afraid to tell Zora when the new job evaporates. He feels so bad about being broke and not being able to treat her on her birthday that his negative attitude spoils the occasion for her as well. Franklin also has not told Zora that he was never officially divorced from his wife. Zora hides these faults from her women friends, but when she and Franklin visit his parents for Thanksgiving, her own big secret—her epilepsy—is revealed. Franklin's mother falls into her usual dysfunctional pattern and throws mashed potatoes in Zora's face. That evening, after Franklin and Zora have gone to bed, she has a seizure.

Shared vulnerabilities draw Franklin and Zora closer. He gives up his room and officially moves in with Zora, but his sporadic employment patterns leave her carrying most of the financial burden. She spends her savings, charges up her credit cards, and borrows money from her father. Her dream of cutting a demo tape and auditioning for a recording contract drifts farther and farther away. When she becomes pregnant with Franklin's child, she makes the painful decision to have an abortion, the third in her life. She does not want to be a single mother, and Franklin's

finances have not brought him any closer tributing to the household expenses.

Zora and Franklin have trouble makin other and their art. When Franklin lands to move to a larger apartment so that he working. Zora diligently works with h hoards money for her demo tape, but ea goal, Franklin seems to fall behind. He ge gets pregnant again and decides she ca abortion.

Franklin had begged Zora not to abor together, but as this pregnancy advances lence. He feels tremendous pressure to fu toward the end of Zora's pregnancy, he Newport Jazz Festival. Anxiety about full jealous fear that Zora will love the baby him in a surly mood guaranteed to spoil In the heat of an argument, Franklin stri

Zora feels too deeply involved to imm ship, but she begins to rely more and m asks a female friend to serve as her Lama she writes many new songs. After the ba izes that she does not have to perform or can reach people with her music. This inner peace that Franklin finds madder attain the same sense of wholeness throu and stops looking for work. He pays no miah. He begins drinking heavily and fi to leave, but, as the time draws near, he When Zora confronts him, he threatens out a restraining order to have him ren fit of fury that she "put the white man the furniture he had built for the apartm for months.

Although the story is not a fairy-tale r tragedy. Franklin reappears after he has self-respect. He returns to apologize to Z the story does not end happily ever afte back to Ohio with her son. However, s popular romance, but in the blues there is a convention that allows male and female singers to take alternate choruses of a song in order to testify about what they have suffered in their relationship.

Blues songs written from a male point of view are often performed by female singers from a female point of view and vice versa. There is also a tradition of "answer songs." A female artist may record a song about her trials with a no-good man only to have a male artist release a response in the voice of the long-suffering lover. Female artists may also respond to songs by male artists, or the original artist of a song that has spawned an "answer" may "answer back" with a new recording. Artists of the same gender may produce answer records in which they portray themselves as romantic rivals of the original artist.

First-person central narration is traditionally the voice of the blues, but the narrative "I" can be inhabited by either gender. Indeed, the function of the blues is testimonial and therefore invites the audience to identify with the emotional experience regardless of the singer's gender or ethnicity. The skillful blues artist must be able to make each member of the audience identify with the experience as his or her own in some measure.

The testimonial function of the narrative further distinguishes *Disappearing Acts* from mainstream popular romance. The function of popular romance is escapism. A well-written story transports the reader into a fantasy realm where the gritty unpleasantness and irritations of daily life do not exist. Popular romance is therefore a nonmimetic form; it does not seek to represent life as it is. Instead, it offers a better reality in which happy endings are the rule. McMillan's blues romance, however, is fully grounded in reality and offers an emotional catharsis rather than an escape. The testimonial format allows every woman who reads the book to relate her own relationship history to Zora's trials with Franklin, while every man who reads the book can identify with moments in his life when it seemed that his best would never be good enough for the woman he loved. Readers can also identify with some of the experiences of the opposite gender character. A woman reader might have been through a long, discouraging job search like Franklin. A male reader might have put his dreams on hold while trying to help someone else the way Zora does.

McMillan does not offer readers a conventional happy ending, but Franklin's final affirmation—"you're the best thing that ever happened to me, and if I . . . lost you, then it's my own damn fault" (367)—does fulfill the customary confession of love romance readers like to hear from the hero in the resolution of the romance. This resolution also echoes titles and phrases from many rhythm and blues songs that are part of the male artist's stock-in-trade. In the blues performance aesthetic, the male singer must be prepared to prove his love by publicly getting down on his knees and begging the object of his affections to remain in his life. Just like the audience at a soul singer's concert, readers who have participated in McMillan's testimonial should be moved to a new level of faith in the power of love. Love may not bring happiness ever after, but it will remain a powerful and enriching bond between Zora and Franklin.

CHARACTER DEVELOPMENT

McMillan's experimentation with multiple protagonists allows readers intimate knowledge of more than one main character. The secondary characters in her novels are usually interesting but not well developed because she concentrates on giving the protagonists so much space to "have their say." Franklin has a violently abusive mother, an alcoholic father, a suicidal sister, and an obese wife from whom he has been separated for years. The poverty of his relationships reflects the scarcity of resources he has to "get his constitution together." In contrast, Zora has a strong social support system. Although her mother died when she was small, she has a loving father and stepmother and three close female friends. Claudette is happily married with children, Portia's hobby is juggling dates, and Marie is struggling to break into the big time as a stand-up comedienne. In McMillan's next novel, *Waiting to Exhale*, a circle of four female friends occupies the narrative center of the story. In *Disappearing Acts*, however, McMillan presents a groundbreaking portrait of an African American couple in love. Given McMillan's role in opening up the marketplace for African American popular romance, it is important to ask how Franklin and Zora anticipate or deviate from the characterization of African American heroes and heroines within the genre.

Idealized Protagonists in African American Popular Romance

Since all romance heroes and heroines are idealized, writers for Arabesque and Indigo, the most successful imprints of "multicultural romance," have used the popular romance form to counter notions that

African Americans, particularly African American men, are not heroic figures. In their guidelines for submissions, both of these presses indicate that they prefer well-educated heroines. Both presses also seek stories about independent women. Thus, their African American heroines are most frequently successful career women who do not need the hero's financial assistance. Indigo specifically states in its submission guidelines, "The hero should be of high status, or high resource, or have the obvious ability to obtain the same." Arabesque does not spell out the hero's qualities this explicitly, but the majority of Arabesque heroes would fulfill Indigo's requirements.

It is precisely this point that makes African American romance heroes more idealized than any other heroes in the romance genre. In real life, there are very few African American men who possess inherited wealth. In contrast, many African American romance heroes are second-or third-generation owners of profitable ranches or corporations. The emphasis on entrepreneurship in these novels is even more distant from reality. The majority of African American millionaires are sports or entertainment figures who have earned their money through their own talent and hard work. Arabesque writers have drawn only a handful of heroes from these fields in a catalogue of over 150 novels. African American romance writers and readers are therefore elaborating a shared vision of racial uplift that casts the heroes and heroines as positive role models.

Judging by Appearances

The integrationist dream of racial equality is for all citizens to be judged by the content of their character, not by the color of their skin. African American popular romance, however, is a cultural nationalist affirmation of a distinct African American identity. Consequently, appearance is the most important aspect of characterization in African American popular romance because it is the first indication that the story is about black people. At the same time, this visual marker has challenged romance publishers to come up with new marketing strategies. Romance readers know what they are looking for and will judge books by their covers, passing over volumes that promise to be too explicit or too tame for their tastes. The mass audience's tendency to judge a book by its cover means that putting black faces on front jackets incurs a risk of losing sales. In 1989, when *Disappearing Acts* first appeared, only one mainstream romance publisher had taken this risk. Four years earlier,

Harlequin had released Sandra Kitt's *Adam and Eva*. Kitt had previously published a Harlequin romance about white characters, but this was the first black romance by a black author in Harlequin's catalogue.

Art directors working for romance publishers have developed a whole code of postures that signal how erotic a book will be even before the reader gets to the plot synopsis on the back jacket. The Synthia St. James painting that graces the cover of *Disappearing Acts* shows a broad-shouldered, dark-brown man gazing down at a chic, medium-brown woman. On the scale of romantic poses, St. James's painting of Franklin and Zora is very tame. Zora stands with her back against Franklin's chest. Both figures are fully clothed. The angle of their heads and cheekbones indicates that they are gazing at each other and smiling broadly, but the narrow V-necked red dress Zora is wearing is the only hint of sensuality in the image. As in all her works, St. James stylizes these human figures so that their forms are represented by solid blocks of color and their faces show no features. Annie Lee and Jonathan Greene are two other African American artists who use stylized, featureless figures in their paintings representing slices of African American life. This technique gives an "everyman" quality to their work, which enables African American viewers to identify closely with their paintings as a documentation of collective African American experience. St. James's depiction of an African American man and woman who delight in each other's presence is therefore a powerful aesthetic statement that perfectly complements McMillan's bold decision to tell the story of an African American man and woman in love.

Zora and Franklin as African American Popular Romance Characters

At first glance, Zora would appear to be the perfect Arabesque or Indigo heroine. When the novel opens, she is about to turn thirty. Heroines in historical novels tend to be in their midtwenties because women married younger in earlier time periods. But contemporary romances usually feature heroines who are between twenty-five and thirty-five. Arabesque heroines often fall at the upper end of this spectrum because Arabesque readers like to identify with heroines who have had time to develop a successful career.

Like most Arabesque and Indigo heroines, Zora has a college degree. As a junior high school music teacher, she shows compassion, fondness for children, and commitment to giving back to her community—all nurturing traits that are admired in romance heroines. Zora's determination to forge a career as a singer/songwriter shows her independence. She is not waiting for a man to complete her or fulfill her dreams. In addition to her drive and strength, however, Zora has likeable vulnerabilities. Her mother died when she was a young girl. The loss of one or both parents is a fairly common trial romance authors assign their heroines in their youth. Such losses make heroines long for solid family ties. They also add human insecurities to the character that make it difficult for her to risk loving and possibly losing again. Such fears enhance dramatic tension in the plot since they stand as internal obstacles on the path toward true love.

Not only has Zora lost her mother, she is also an epileptic. Her condition challenges the physical perfection usually expected of heroines, but deep unmentionable secrets are another humanizing device romance authors use to add internal obstacles to the progress of the love affair. Another one of Zora's secret insecurities is that she used to be fat. When Franklin sees a photograph of her from her pre–Weight Watchers days, she lies and says it is a picture of her mother. Still, Zora satisfies the most important requirement for a romance heroine: she is beautiful. McMillan, like subsequent African American romance authors, is careful to cast Zora's beauty in terms of an Afro-centric aesthetic. She is tall and brown-skinned. Carrying 140 voluptuous pounds on her five-foot eight-inch frame, she is not fashion-model svelte, but Franklin, like most African American men, appreciates her generous curves. As the saying goes in the African American community, "Don't nobody but a dog want a bone." Arabesque has gone so far as to experiment with expressing this aesthetic on its covers. Leslie Esdaile's *Sundance*, for instance, published in 1996, features a full-figured model in a midriff-baring top. Overall, African American popular romance writers seek to show that beauty comes in a variety of sizes as well as colors.

McMillan uses Franklin's point of view to present most of the details about Zora's appearance. This device enables her to simultaneously characterize Franklin through his response to Zora's appearance. The first thing he notices is her grace, saying that she moves like a gazelle (37). Next he mentions her "pretty brown eyes" (40). One page later, Franklin finds himself lost in contemplation because the smooth wood he had been polishing reminds him of Zora's skin. Not until eight pages later does he mention her breasts and derriere. Consequently, readers see that Franklin is attracted to Zora as a whole person. The impressions he collects as he helps her settle into her apartment convey even more admiration for her character. Zora decorates her home tastefully with original artworks by African American artists. Her quality stereo system, extensive album collection, and shelves of books indicate that she is a cultured person. It is easy for readers to understand why Franklin falls for her.

On the surface, it is also easy to understand why Zora falls for Franklin. When Zora meets him for the first time, she is struck dumb (24). McMillan uses Zora's point of view to describe Franklin's appearance with an African American woman's appreciation for his "dark," "handsome" features. Zora notes that his nose is "strong and regal," his lips are "succulent," and his muscular arms are "the color of black grapes" (25). With this assessment, McMillan turns all the racial traits that have stereotypically been denigrated as ugly into the hallmarks of Franklin's beauty.

Still, McMillan is writing realist rather than idealistic fiction. As such, her African American hero is a common laborer. Whereas the ideal heroes of Arabesque and Indigo novels typically own well-appointed condos, four-bedroom suburban houses, or family mansions, Franklin rents a room from week to week and is months behind in his rent when he meets Zora. Whereas most Arabesque and Indigo heroes drive powerful, luxurious automobiles as symbols of their financial success, Franklin has no car. Worse, whereas medical doctors, attorneys, and business executives abound in the world of African American popular romance, Franklin has only a hard-earned general equivalency diploma.

If McMillan had provided the story with a happy ending in which Franklin ultimately became "powerful" and reached "high status regardless of his initial circumstances" (per Indigo's submission guidelines), he might have met the criteria of the typical black romance hero. However, he does exhibit great intelligence. Despite his lack of formal education, he has read more widely than Zora. He has an extensive vocabulary and can beat her at Scrabble any day. Unfortunately, the fact that he has never formally divorced his wife and does not reveal this information to Zora until after they have become lovers would strike romance readers as despicably dishonest. Romance heroes are permitted sexual outlets, but prior legal or emotional commitments disqualify a character from starring opposite the heroine.

Zora too falls short of the ideal in the area of her past relationships. Although romance heroines are no longer bound to be virgins, readers prefer that their experience not be too expansive. Yet, early in the book, Zora kisses and tells in explicit detail, describing five lovers and two abortions (17–20). In contrast, popular romance writers seek to create the illusion that everything feels pure and new even if it is not the heroine's first time falling in love. Details about previous relationships tend to destroy this illusion and may cause readers to reject the heroine as a "promiscuous" woman.

McMillan's characterization of Franklin and Zora anticipates subsequent African American popular romance writers' efforts to celebrate Afro-centric standards of beauty. Zora also exhibits many of the admirable characteristics with which the emerging audience of middle-class African American readers enjoys identifying. Yet McMillan's artistic aim is different from that of most African American popular romance writers. She seeks to represent black life as it is. African American popular romance depicts black life as readers like to believe it could be. This difference accounts for Franklin's "failure" as a romance hero.

CULTURAL CONTEXT

Franklin as John Henry, the Archetypal African American Working Man

Although Franklin does not pass muster as an idealized romance hero, he is modeled on one of the greatest African American folk heroes— John Henry. The legend of John Henry describes him as an extraordinarily strong "steel driving man." John Henry worked for the railroads, driving the steel spikes used to anchor railroad track. His broad shoulders, deep barrel chest, and powerful arms enabled him to hammer the spikes into place faster than any man alive. Then came the day when the railroad company brought in a steam drill to drive spikes faster and more efficiently than human beings. The legend of John Henry expressed black workers' resentment at being displaced by new technologies in the late nineteenth and early twentieth centuries. John Henry refused to acknowledge the superiority of the machine. He challenged the steam drill to a contest and actually proved he could drive spikes faster than it could. Unfortunately, he died as a result of this Herculean effort. Nevertheless, on the threshold of the twenty-first century, workers can still ruefully identify with the experience of being replaced by machines. Thus, the legend of John Henry lives on.

When Zora first sees Franklin, he is wielding John Henry's ubiquitous tool: "I looked down, saw a curved red back, then a long arm flying up, thick black fingers grasping a hammer" (24). The evening after he helps Zora set up her apartment, Franklin returns to his room and tries to work on a tree stump he is shaping into a table. The action of pushing his gouge through the soft wood expresses his desire to make love with Zora. Similarly, the legend of John Henry swinging his steel hammer in the railroad tunnel has always resonated with sexual innuendo. Lost in his reverie, Franklin tries to reason with himself, "Franklin, can't you hear that train coming man?" (52). Here he refers to a folk saying that falling in love feels like getting hit by a freight train.

Yet Franklin is no more able to avoid his destiny than was John Henry, who knew, even as a baby, that "a hammer be the death of me." By the end of the evening, Franklin's feet are covered with wood shavings, but "I didn't feel no railroad tracks underneath 'em, so I kicked most of 'em off and fell across the bed" (52). The railroad imagery continues the allusion to John Henry, who stands as the epitome of "a natural man" in African American folk culture. By aligning Franklin with the John Henry myth, then, McMillan effectively uses his struggle to highlight the challenges that African American men have faced as laborers throughout their history in the United States.

Many of the African captives brought to the United States were already skilled craftsmen when they arrived. Carpenters, joiners, blacksmiths, goldsmiths, master weavers, leather workers, and many other artisans flourished in African societies. In the United States, masters often apprenticed talented slaves so that they could learn a trade. Large plantations were like factories, producing a variety of goods, and required skilled workers to keep the buildings and machinery in good repair. Slave artisans also crafted many household goods, such as furniture, clothing, and shoes. When their services were not needed, masters could hire out skilled slaves at a profit. Some permitted such slaves to keep a portion of their earnings. Hence, skilled slaves had more opportunity than most to save enough money to purchase their freedom. In the late eighteenth and early nineteenth centuries, free blacks dominated many trades in such cities as Charleston and New Orleans. Franklin's talent for woodworking therefore connects him with a heritage that reaches back to Africa.

Political upheaval and famine brought a deluge of new European immigrants to the United States in the mid-nineteenth century. Their numbers swelled the labor force and increased competition for jobs. Very quickly foreign-born whites and native-born whites closed ranks in solidarity and began pushing black workers out of the higher-paying skilled jobs. Thus, from its beginnings, the labor movement in the United States has been tainted with the same racist ideology that pervaded the larger society.

African-American Workers and the Labor Movement

Black workers have historically demonstrated enthusiasm for the concept of collective bargaining; however, African Americans also preserve bitter memories of discriminatory union policies. Early union organizers often wrote bylaws into the union constitutions excluding blacks from membership. In some industries, unions pursued a deliberate policy of driving black workers out of professions they had dominated for generations. In other cases, union leaders encouraged black workers to form their own segregated locals. This practice resulted in separate and unequal lines of seniority, with white workers always being given preference over blacks in hiring and promotion. Toward the end of the nineteenth century, the Noble Order of the Knights of Labor integrated blacks and whites, males and females, and skilled and unskilled workers into its ranks. Unfortunately, this organization lost credibility after the Haymarket Riot in 1886.

As the labor movement gained more power, employers began using black workers as strikebreakers. This practice exacerbated tensions between white and black workers, but black workers were grateful for the chance to earn wages that far outstripped what they could hope to make under the sharecropping system. Hours were long, and working conditions were dangerous, but black workers also had little reason to feel solidarity with striking union workers because most unions did not admit blacks.

In the early twentieth century, union leaders began to realize that alienating black workers diminished their own power. The Congress of Industrial Organizations (CIO) united workers in the steel, auto, mining, meatpacking, and rubber industries. Most of these plants were located in the North. Black workers who had begun to head northward as part of the Great Migration were employed in these industries in large numbers. The CIO erased segregationist bylaws from its constitutions in these industries but was never able to effectively enforce its antidiscrimination policy among the locals. Thus, even during World War II, when manufacturing was a critical part of the war effort, factory owners were reluctant to hire black workers, and white workers often refused to work with blacks.

A. Philip Randolph, leader of the Brotherhood of Sleeping Car Porters (the most powerful black union in the country), threatened to organize a march on Washington, D.C., to protest these discriminatory practices. When this idea came to fruition twenty years later under the leadership of Dr. Martin Luther King, Jr., and the Southern Christian Leadership Conference, it was a triumphant demonstration of human fellowship without regard for race, color, or creed. During the war years, however, a civil rights march on Washington would have been an international embarrassment. President Franklin Roosevelt forestalled such protest by signing an executive order mandating that all employers with federal contracts had to abide by the principle of equal opportunity in hiring. Even then, black workers were relegated to the dirtiest, most dangerous jobs.

As agitation for full civil rights increased in the postwar years, many craft and hall locals in the South became allied with segregationists. It was not uncommon for a White Citizens Council or the Ku Klux Klan to meet in union halls. Consequently, black workers in the South tended to vote in a block against unionization when organizers came to the plants where they worked. Still, civil rights leaders and union leaders formed an uneasy alliance in the late 1950s and early 1960s. Together, their constituents helped elect John F. Kennedy to the presidency. Unfortunately, after the passage of the civil right legislation of 1964 and 1965, this alliance began to dissolve. Most of the civil rights leaders came from an intellectual elite. Their focus on desegregation in schools, housing, transportation, and restaurants did not address the most pressing concerns of blue-collar workers. Riots in urban ghettos brought some of the entrenched economic injustices to the fore, but they also distracted black leadership from their coalition with labor leaders.

At the same time, labor leaders failed to follow through on their pledges to eliminate racism in unions. Instead, they found their constituents drifting away from the Democratic Party to join the Republican backlash against "Great Society" and affirmative action programs. Eventually, these new Republicans helped put Ronald Reagan in office. When *Disappearing Acts* opens, it is 1982, two years into Reagan's first term. The country is deep in an economic recession. Franklin's struggle to get his "constitution" together represents the whole history of black men trying to get an honest day's pay for an honest day's work under a national constitution that originally counted them as only three-fifths of a human being.

The fact that Franklin has chosen to work in the building trades makes his struggle even more difficult. Historically, the building trades have been among the highest paying in private industry. Since training for these jobs has usually required only a minimum of education, they have served as sturdy stepping-stones into middle-class affluence for many immigrant workers. Yet the way the building trades are organized has made it especially difficult for black workers to penetrate their ranks. During the Great Depression, the building trade unions decided to protect their members by keeping the number of skilled workers low. By limiting the number of apprentices who could be trained as electricians, plumbers, pipe fitters, and the like, they kept wages high. Since the union had so much power to decide who could be trained for these jobs, it was naturally very easy to keep blacks out.

Most construction jobs are also filled at the discretion of the local unions, not employers. Thus, when a contractor needs workers for a job, the union, in theory, contacts the members who are at the top of a rotating list and sends them to the job site. In practice, it is also easy for locals to give preference to some members over others, so that even when blacks have been able to join these unions, they still have not always had an equal chance at the available jobs.

For these reasons, blacks had been picketing construction sites since the 1960s. Construction declined nationwide during the 1970s but remained strong in New York City, where *Disappearing Acts* takes place. By the early 1980s, black and Hispanic workers who wanted construction jobs had built up years of frustration. In the climate of increased economic uncertainty caused by the recession, they channeled their frustrations into organizing larger demonstrations at construction sites in the city. On July 20, 1981, one such demonstration turned violent. Eight hundred unemployed black and Hispanic workers fought with construction workers at two sites. It took 325 police officers to quell the riot. Twenty-five workers and twelve police officers were hospitalized due to injuries sustained during the disturbance (Ploski and Williams 562).

Franklin's quest for an honest day's work takes place shortly after this uprising, in a climate where city officials have nominally acceded to demands for equal racial and ethnic representation on job sites. Unions and contractors, however, remain unwilling to honor the concept of "equal opportunity." Thus, for most of the novel, Franklin is able to find only short-term work as a laborer.

Before desegregation, limited educational opportunities and discriminatory hiring practices had kept most blacks out of white-collar employment. Employers and unions had also colluded to keep blacks out of higher-paying skilled jobs. Therefore, until the time of the generation that came of age with desegregation, most blacks had no choice but to work as unskilled laborers, regardless of their talents. African Americans born during the baby boom years who completed college degrees have experienced unprecedented opportunities to advance in the working world. Thus, Zora is secure in her career as a teacher, and she can afford to dream about succeeding as an artist. Black baby boomers like Franklin who did not complete college, however, have experienced increasing economic hardship.

In the 1970s and 1980s, unskilled black workers were disproportionately affected by sweeping changes in the American economy. Improved technology enabled employers to phase out many unskilled jobs. More black workers were clustered in those kinds of jobs, so more black workers suddenly found themselves out of work. Lacking skills and education, they also had difficulty finding new jobs in an economy where the need for unskilled labor was shrinking. Meanwhile, American businesses had to complete in an increasingly global market. Seeking ways to cut costs, they began shipping manufacturing overseas to countries with a lower standard of living.

Back home, corporations began "downsizing" their labor forces. These cuts also affected black workers disproportionately because years of discriminatory hiring and promotion practices had left them with less seniority. The last hired were usually the first fired. All of these factors combined to create epidemic rates of unemployment for African American men. In 1980, white male unemployment was 4.4 percent, while black male unemployment was 9.6 percent. In 1990, the year after *Disappearing Acts* was published, white male unemployment was 4 percent, while black male unemployment was 8.6 percent (Smith and Horton 592). For most of thirty-four-year-old Franklin's working life, his statistical chance of being unemployed was at least 2.3 times greater than a white man's. It was Franklin's choice to drop out of school instead of preparing himself for a career as Zora did. Nevertheless, his disaffection accurately expresses the sentiments of many men in his generation, and his attitude is understandable in light of the historic pressures black men have faced in America.

In effect, historical experience in the United States had challenged African American men to forge a new definition of manhood, one that must extend beyond financial security for the family. African American romance writers are currently elaborating a vision in which tall, dark, and handsome heroes can own their own corporations and fly around the world in private jets. Conversely, McMillan explores how the economic realities of racism affect an African American couple who are trying to love and honor each other. Her examination of these socioeconomic conditions in the context of relationships is typical of the way that contemporary black women writers have developed their political commentary on the status of blacks in the United States. The fact that McMillan decided to tell a love story instead of writing a societal protest novel does not mean her work is devoid of political consciousness.

THEMATIC ISSUES: THE ARTISTIC PROCESS

While McMillan establishes a direct link with Zora Neale Hurston, her blues romance, *Disappearing Acts*, shares many elements of its thematic organization with James Baldwin's earlier love story, *If Beale Street Could Talk*. Both stories take place in New York City. Franklin and Zora live in Brooklyn, while Baldwin's protagonists, Fonnie and Tish, had grown up together in Harlem. They are on the brink of getting married and moving to an apartment in Greenwich Village when Fonnie is falsely accused of rape and incarcerated in the Tombs. His imprisonment symbolizes the plight of all black men in America, just as Franklin's inability to hold a job symbolizes the economic pressures that all black men face in America. Both Baldwin and McMillan detail how the impact of these external pressures affects relationships between African American men and women.

Fonnie and Franklin both come from dysfunctional families. They both have emotionally abusive mothers. They also both have two sisters. Fonnie's sisters are light-skinned like their mother and share her disdain for him. Franklin's mother favors his sister Cynthia but rejects his sister Darlene. Fonnie shares a close bond with his father, but Frank is a weak man who allows his wife's temper to rule the household. He drinks to escape the discord in his home. Franklin's father is similarly weak and also escapes from reality through the means of alcohol. Fortunately for Fonnie, his sweetheart, Tish, comes from a loving, supportive family. While growing up, he spent more time in her home than in his own. Likewise, although her mother died when she was small, Zora's father and stepmother gave her ample love and support. They also provided enough material resources to get her through college. When Franklin and Zora visit her parents over Christmas, they welcome him as warmly as Tish's family welcomes Fonnie. The most important similarity between these two blues romances, however, is the central role Baldwin and McMillan give the theme of artistic creation.

Fonnie is a talented sculptor. Like most of the young men in his neighborhood, he did not care much for school, but when he began to study woodworking, he discovered his vocation. Franklin also found school boring but never missed a wood-shop class. Fonnie carves statues and figurines, while Franklin crafts handmade furniture, but Baldwin and McMillan show both characters actively engaged in their artistic process throughout their novels. Yet Baldwin does not give Tish a creative vocation. She hypothesizes, "perhaps Fonnie saved me because he was just about the only boy I knew who wasn't fooling around with needles or drinking cheap wine or mugging people or holding up stores" (39). Her mother had been a singer, but Tish's role in the novel is to bear Fonnie's child and keep him from succumbing to despair while he is in prison.

If Beale Street Could Talk is not an antifeminist text. Tish recounts the story as a first-person central narrator. The novel's title refers to a famous blues song by W. C. Handy. The song's lyrics catalogue all the sights one can see on the famous Beale Street in Memphis. In typical blues fashion, this song implies that real wisdom comes from absorbing life experiences. If Beale Street could talk, it would tell profound truths about human nature. Loving a black man in the United States, nineteen-year-old Tish has experienced enough trouble to gain a respectable amount of wisdom. Her narrative functions in a blues testimonial mode that serves to impart this wisdom to others. Within the blues tradition, this process of testifying is a process of artistic creation. Thus, while Tish does not identify herself as an artist, she does engage in creative process. Tish, her mother, and her sister are also strong, admirable female characters. Yet McMillan's novel effectively revises Baldwin's blues romance by providing the heroine with her own artistic pursuits, in the form of Zora's aspirations.

In fact, where Fonnie and Tish are separated only by external forces, one of the most difficult issues for Zora and Franklin to resolve is how to make room in their lives for each other without diminishing their art. At first, Zora and Franklin appreciate each other as kindred spirits. As Franklin says, "me and Zora dream together" (110). He is proud to be with such a talented woman. He understands her obsession with her music because he knows that he gets just as absorbed in his woodwork.

Zora is grateful for his supportive attitude, but when he gives up his room and moves in with her, she laments that "there was no way this would feel like my sanctuary now" (176). Ultimately, although his finances are precarious, Franklin pushes for them to get a larger apartment because he would like to have a work space where he can leave sawdust on the floor. Yet the added expense increases the pressure on Franklin to be more successful as a breadwinner. When Zora becomes pregnant, Franklin suffers even more anxiety.

After her third abortion, Zora has a nightmare that the doctors have removed her voice along with the fetus: "Is this how much a baby costs?" she asks (147). When she conceives a fourth time, she cannot bring herself to terminate the pregnancy again. Still, she fears that motherhood will hamper her musical career. If nothing else, the added expenses will make it more difficult for her to save money to rent studio time and cut a demo tape. Indeed, it seems that each time she moves a step closer to her professional goals, Franklin's financial problems cause her to fall two steps back. For example, when Zora is invited to audition with an R&B band, instead of sharing her enthusiasm, Franklin is preoccupied because he has just been released from his most recent construction job. Instead of offering his support, he claims that he might be too tired out from work to accompany her to the audition. Knowing that their finances are shaky, Zora's father gives each of them $500 for Christmas, but they end up arguing about this money. Franklin wants to pool their funds and purchase a car. Zora insists on saving hers to pay for her demo tape. Franklin begins to resent the fact that Zora puts her art ahead of him. After their son is born, he fears that the baby also means more to Zora than he does.

Despite her fear that motherhood will keep her from achieving her artistic goals, Zora finds . . . that, since becoming pregnant, her creative powers have heightened and that she has been able to write several good songs. After the baby arrives, leaving him in day care when her maternity leave runs out is emotionally difficult for Zora. Working full-time, managing the household, and caring for her son is physically draining— especially since Franklin hangs around the house all day but refuses to look for a job or assist Zora. Still, Zora does not give up her artistic goals. She merely revises them.

Motherhood as she envisions it does not fit comfortably with her dream of succeeding as a singer. She cannot imagine either leaving her son behind or dragging him along on concert tours. Instead, she realizes, "not only can you sing, Zora, but you can *write*" (330). With this epiphany, Zora grows into full artistic maturity. Unfortunately, Franklin is not able to find a similar sense of fulfillment in his woodworking. He sinks into what might be described as a postpartum depression. He begins drinking heavily and suffers an injury on the job due to his intoxication. Zora provides him with funds to purchase quality materials, and he spends several months sequestered in their apartment building a custom bookcase and bed.

Their relationship continues to deteriorate, however, and after Franklin threatens her with violence, Zora secures a restraining order against him that requires that he vacate the apartment. In a fit of rage, Franklin then destroys the furniture he had so meticulously crafted and smashes everything he and Zora had acquired together. Franklin had felt threatened by Zora's determination to prove herself a superwoman. He acknowledges that she is a good mother and that she pays all the bills, but he resists what he sees as her calculated effort to show him up by saying, "I'ma get a job, but when I feel like it. She pressuring me all the time, and it seem like the more she get on my case, the less I feel like doing" (332). He seems even more threatened by the fact that she is writing songs again. His words suggest that Zora's ability to exercise both generative and artistic power makes him feel inadequate. Perhaps this is why James Baldwin did not endow Tish with an artistic vocation. The final lines of his novel conflate Fonnie's creative work with Tish's pro-creative labor: "Fonnie is working on the wood, on the stone, whistling, smiling. And, from far away, but coming nearer, the baby cries and cries and cries and cries and cries and cries and cries and cries, cries like it means to wake the dead." (213).

Symbolically, then, their baby is more the product of Fonnie's artistic vision than Tish's reproductive labor. Franklin also equates his woodwork with his son, saying they are the only things he has made lately of which he is proud. McMillan, however, does not make Jeremiah into an abstract symbol like Fonnie and Tish's baby. Pregnancy inspires Zora to write more songs, but childbearing and artistic creation are not substitutes for each other from her point of view.

ALTERNATIVE INTERPRETATION: SOCIAL REALISM

In the early twentieth century, the Communist Party began encouraging writers and visual artists to use their talents to raise the political consciousness of the masses and thereby help engage them in the project of socialist revolution. Socialist realism was the official aesthetic of the Soviet Union from 1932 until the mid-1980s. Novelist Maksim Gorki helped define the socialist realist method when he became the founding president of the Union of Soviet Writers in 1934. He believed that art should depict society in its revolutionary development, hence its purpose should be to inspire the masses. Yet the term remained vague, and many writers and artists inadvertently incurred the displeasure of Communist Party officials even when they were fully committed to using their art to stir the masses.

One of the key difficulties in the socialist realist aesthetic is its inherent tension between idealism and realism. On the one hand, socialist realism demands that the artist depict the evils of class warfare in gritty detail. On the other hand, the socialist realist aesthetic requires that the artist present idealized heroes who exemplify the virtues of the revolutionary worker. Since socialist realist fiction seeks to illustrate the impact of historical forces on whole groups of people, socialist realist writers have frequently presented individual characters as larger-than-life symbols for a collective experience. As a result, heroes and other characters in socialist realist literature often strike critics as two-dimensional types rather than as believable human beings. Socialist realist writers have had a difficult time making readers care about and empathize with their protagonists. Worse, writers who have tried to humanize their characters by evoking the cultural-specific setting in which they move have been regularly criticized for subordinating the reality of class warfare to ethnic and racial tensions. Thus, the tension between socialist ideals and black writers' lived experience frequently exacerbated the double consciousness dilemma W.E.B. Du Bois had outlined in *The Souls of Black Folk*.

Compared to the social protests against racial injustice lodged by Richard Wright, Ralph Ellison, and James Baldwin, McMillan's deft use of the romance plot to protest the intersection of race, class, and gender oppression is a significant formal innovation. Her insistence on portraying black love in a realist rather than an idealist mode also sets her apart from the aims of African American popular romance writers. Yet the "revolutionary romance" is a well-established form in the larger framework of Pan-African literatures. *Disappearing Acts* clearly promotes a functionalist definition of art both in its presentation of the dual protagonists as artists and in the conception of its romance plot as a vehicle for social protest. Consequently, it is reasonable to place McMillan's approach to social protest writing within a wider context than the African American experience in the United States. Since the international community of black writers had been deeply influenced by socialist realism, it also makes sense to ask how well McMillan's vision of art's functional purpose in society fits this revolutionary definition of art.

Pan-African Social Protest Writing

Marxist analysis of economic exploitation of workers had appealed to a Pan-African cross section of twentieth-century black writers because it offers an ideological framework for protesting the plight of the individual within a broader struggle between the haves and the have-nots. Indeed W. E. B. Du Bois joined the Communist Party at the end of his life and renounced his U.S. citizenship to die as a citizen of the newly independent Ghana. Nonetheless, many black writers have found it difficult to force their creative vision to fit the demands of socialist realism. For instance, Jacques Roumain's 1944 novel *Masters of the Dew* is a definitive example of a black writer's difficulties in producing socialist realist fiction acceptable to the international Communist Party.

Roumain came from an elite family in Haiti but joined the Communist Party as a young man and devoted his life to bringing about a more equitable distribution of wealth in the country. His peasant novel provides a detailed portrait of life in a rural Haitian village, and its "creolized" French narrative reflects the rhythms and syntax of the Haitian Creole language. The novel was so widely admired throughout the international community of black writers that Langston Hughes and Mercer Cook translated it into English in 1947. Unfortunately, party officials disapproved of *Masters of the Dew* because they felt Roumain's emphasis on cultural nationalism had subordinated class warfare to racial politics.

Despite Marxist disapproval, Roumain's novel provides a pattern one would expect African American writers to emulate: the allegorical use of romantic love to symbolize the birth of a new social order. It is intriguing that most black American writers have not made similar use of romance plots in social protest fiction. Perhaps it has been difficult for African American writers in the United States to imagine the birth of a black nation while living as a minority population "in the belly of the beast." However, McMillan, like Roumain, makes effective use of the romance plot as a vehicle for social protest. Her attempts to imagine the flowering of black-on-black love in *Disappearing Acts* and *How Stella Got Her Groove Back* mark an important new development in African American fiction. The avid response her novels and African American popular romance novels have generated indicates that the imagined community of African American readers is hungry for visions of black-on-black love either as it is or as it could be. Significantly, both visions hinge on a redefinition of African American manhood.

The Socialist Realist Hero

On the surface, McMillan's decision to model Franklin after John Henry would seem to cast him as a perfect socialist realist hero. Within the terms of a Marxist ideology, John Henry's struggle against the machine vividly dramatizes the revolutionary worker's struggle against oppressive capitalism. The story of John Henry can also illustrate the Marxist view that capitalist overlords devalue the dignity of labor and seek to turn all workers into subhuman robots even when they do not directly replace them with machines. In a Marxist analysis, the fact that John Henry was a railroad worker is also significant because railroad ushered in the era of rapid transit that facilitated the organization of an industrial capitalist economy. Thus, John Henry symbolically struggles against all the injustices inherent in the process of industrialization. Finally, with his muscles rippling under his faded overalls, John Henry is a romantic figure whose ability to best the machine raises him to superhuman stature.

While party officials did not want writers to emphasize racial or ethnic tensions over class warfare, judicious use of authentic folk heroes was encouraged and applauded. McMillan's choice of John Henry as Franklin's model offers African American readers a figure they can identify with directly, while his example can inspire all the workers of the world. Better still, within the African American performance aesthetic, the legend of John Henry is the story of a culture hero whose exploits symbolize a collective experience. Thus, he is especially suited to interpretation as a socialist hero who works for the common good rather than for individual advancement. Folklorists often point out that one of the distinguishing traits of African American folk culture is to celebrate communal heroes as opposed to individualistic "heroes of exaggeration," such as Paul Bunyan. McMillan follows this tradition by making Franklin's narrative "I" function in a blues testimonial mode. In this way, she deliberately invites her audience to accept his testimony as a collective history, just as the story of John Henry expresses a collective experience.

Indeed, McMillan makes ironic commentary on the Paul Bunyan myth

cycle and its celebration of individual advancement when Franklin reflects on the market value of his strength. He comments that he can
always hear employers thinking "that nigger looks like Paul Bunyan.
Take him" (104). Physically, like the mythical lumberjack, Franklin is
larger than life. The irony is that his size and strength do not endow him
with comparable power to make his mark on the American landscape.
Instead, like John Henry, he is doomed to pit his strength against the
dehumanizing political and economic machinery of the country only to
go down in tragic defeat. When Franklin is fired from the job he had
thought would finally enable him to earn union membership, he discovers that the organization that had supposedly been helping minority
workers land construction jobs had actually been accepting payoffs to
keep blacks and Hispanics off job sites. McMillan draws the name of this
organization, A Dream Deferred, from the title of a famous collection of
poems by Langston Hughes. In doing so, she calls on Hughes's lifelong
blues testimonial about the trials of working-class blacks and uses the
reference to expose the corrupt system that keeps men like Franklin from
realizing their dreams.

Each time Franklin expresses his desire to get his "constitution" together, McMillan delivers sharp jabs at the popular myth that thrift and
industry inevitably lead to success in American society. Her Franklin is
ironically named after Benjamin Franklin, one of the framers of the U.S.
Constitution, who helped promote the virtues of thrift and industry in
his *Poor Richard's Almanac*. Yet, prior to the Thirteenth, Fourteenth, and
Fifteenth Amendments, the U.S. Constitution explicitly excluded African
Americans from reaping the benefits of their labor. McMillan's realistic
depiction of black urban life further signifies the discrepancy between
the American faith in individual advancement through thrift and industry and the near impossibility of exercising those virtues under the economic reality most African Americans have faced. Ann Petry, an earlier
best-selling African American woman novelist, had woven a similar critique of Benjamin Franklin's ideals into her 1946 novel *The Street*. Lutie
Johnson, the novel's protagonist, overhears stock tips and "thrift and
industry" maxims while working as a maid. When she tries to apply
these virtues in her own life, however, she always comes up "a day late
and a dollar short."

In many ways, Petry's novel is a response to Richard Wright's *Native
Son*. It articulates an African American female approach to social protest.
McMillan shows similar concern for incorporating an African American
female point of view into the social protest tradition in *Disappearing Acts*.

As Zora says, "the saddest thing in the world is to see your man out of work" (143). Franklin desperately needs a "new deal" such as the one ostensibly offered by his other namesake, President Franklin Delano Roosevelt, during the Great Depression. Instead, he continues to receive the same "raw deal" that has been the lot of African American workers throughout their history in the United States. McMillan therefore implicitly protests economic injustice by ironically naming her hero after two political figures whose best efforts still failed to alleviate the plight of black Americans.

Here, however, like the writers who were censured for focusing too much on racial or ethnic tensions, McMillan further transgresses the ideological aims of socialist realism by offering an analysis of gender politics along with her protest against economic injustice. While McMillan critiques a constellation of race, class, and gender oppressions, socialist realist doctrine would assert that the representation of racism and sexism in her characters' lives should remain secondary to issues of class warfare. But by giving Zora equal time to testify instead of focusing only on Franklin's struggle, McMillan causes him to fail both as a romance hero and as a socialist realist hero.

Above all, the socialist realist hero must be a moral figure. He may be forced to make difficult sacrifices for the sake of the revolution, but his actions must exemplify the virtues of socialist leadership. In contrast, Franklin leaves his wife and essentially abandons his sons, not for the sake of a political activism, which dictates that "the needs of the many outweigh the needs of the few," but because he has accepted the consumerist belief that he cannot be a good husband and father if he cannot afford to give his family expensive things. Zora shoulders the full burden of providing for the son she conceives with Franklin, while he loafs at home and refuses even to pick up their child from day care because people will know he does not have a job if he has time to spend with his son in the middle of the day. Both Franklin and Zora assert that the yardstick that measures a man by how much money he makes measures wrongly. McMillan's skillful characterization enables readers to understand Franklin's motivations and empathize with him as a human being. Nevertheless, when they hear Zora's testimony about how his actions affect her, they cannot see him as an idealized hero.

Consequently, while McMillan's blues aesthetic has some points of convergence with the aims of socialist realism, overall *Disappearing Acts* does not satisfy a socialist realist aesthetic. Both the blues and the socialist realist aesthetic can yield gritty representations of economic injustice. The blues aesthetic also privileges a functionalist vision of art. Franklin's craftsmanship would fulfill a socialist realist aesthetic because he takes pride in creating objects for everyday use. The blues aesthetic, however, is part of an African-derived cosmology which recognizes a spiritual dimension in even the most mundane tasks. The blues aesthetic has been relegated to the "secular" realm in American life, but within this mode, it is quite natural for Zora to envision her art touching people's spirits and uplifting them, whether her voice is ringing out in church or accompanying them on cassettes as they drive down the highway. Although some revolutionary leaders like Haiti's Jean-Bertrand Aristide have combined Marxist analysis with spiritual faith to create a powerful liberation theology, in general Marxism does not recognize this spiritual dimension of life. Thus, in a socialist realist view, Zora's music could only "uplift" the masses by increasing their zeal for revolutionary insurgency.

The blues aesthetic favors a very realistic mode of representing the world, but the reality the blues transmit is distinctly an African-American one. McMillan's formal and thematic articulation of blues romance promotes a cultural nationalist consciousness instead of Marxist revolutionary consciousness. The worldview she represents in the text regards racism, sexism, and economic discrimination as an interlocking nexus of oppressions. Hence, in a socialist realist interpretation of the text, McMillan's ideological orientation would constitute a serious flaw because she does not portray class warfare as the primary locus of social inequity.

McMillan's Own Style of Social Protest

McMillan, like many contemporary African American women writers, has another agenda apart from that of the traditional social protest orientation. She departs from the tradition by critiquing "black macho" as a threat to the collective struggle for civil liberties. Ultimately, Franklin fails as both a romance hero and as a socialist realist hero because he attempts to define manhood as a position of dominance over women. When Zora appears to have outgrown him, he threatens her with physical violence, forces her to have sex against her will, and refuses to let her get up to wash afterward, saying, "I want you to sleep in it, so you'll know you slept with a real man all night" (336). This scene, like numerous other scenes of black male domestic violence in black women's fiction, symbolizes the corruption of personal liberty. Franklin "disappears" as a human being because he fails to take responsibility for his own life. Further, for as long as Zora tries to assume responsibility for him, her own power wanes. *Disappearing Acts* therefore calls for a new paradigm of black male/female relationships in addition to indicting the political and economic oppression under which African Americans live. By daring to follow her own aesthetic vision, McMillan paints a masterful portrait of two complex human beings, overturning pernicious stereotypes about black love and black sexuality in the process.

5

Waiting to Exhale
(1992)

The unprecedented commercial success of *Waiting to Exhale* awakened the publishing and film industries to the lucrative market for stories that reflect the lifestyles and concerns of middle-class African American women. From the beginning of her career, McMillan had cultivated an intimate relationship with this audience of her upwardly mobile sisters. In *Waiting to Exhale*, McMillan cemented her bond with this core audience of African American women and successfully attracted a crossover audience. The key to her wide-ranging appeal is her skill in adapting the conventional forms and themes of mainstream popular women's fiction to reflect an African American worldview. McMillan structured *Waiting to Exhale* in the classic four-woman form pioneered by Louisa May Alcott in *Little Women*. *Waiting to Exhale*'s familiar four-woman structure and its focus on themes of particular concern to women (most notably, the shortage of marriageable men) touched a broad spectrum of readers across race, class, and culture.

PLOT DEVELOPMENT

Like all of McMillan's novels, *Waiting to Exhale* does not exhibit a traditional plot structured around a central conflict between a single protagonist and the people or forces that oppose his or her goals. While

Mama and *Disappearing Acts* both feature dual protagonists, *Waiting to Exhale* presents one year in the lives of four women who live in Phoenix, Arizona. In *Waiting to Exhale*, McMillan balances four main characters— Savannah, Bernadine, Gloria, and Robin—but Savannah emerges as the strongest character in the book. Her first-person narration engages the reader more intimately than the third-person narration that presents Bernadine and Gloria. Savannah also shows more self-awareness than any of the other characters. She is not immune to making foolish choices, but, unlike Gloria, she is willing to risk making mistakes, and, unlike Robin, she is able to take responsibility for her actions and learn from her experiences. Savannah's desire for a life partner is one with which the majority of readers can identify. Yet McMillan does not make winning or losing in the game of love the central element of Savannah's story line. What Savannah learns about herself along the way is far more important. Thus, the day she tells her mother to "butt out" of her romantic life and hangs up the phone on her married suitor marks significant growth for her.

Savannah Jackson is new to town. She moves to Phoenix shortly after the New Year, hoping to find greater fulfillment in her career as well as in her romantic life. Savannah had been earning $50,000 per year as a public relations officer for the gas company in Denver, Colorado. She accepts a $12,000 pay cut to work for a television station in Phoenix because she might have a chance to produce television shows about issues affecting the African American community.

Savannah helps support her mother because her father deserted his wife and children over seventeen years before. Although Savannah is a successful college graduate, her siblings have not been as fortunate. One brother is in jail. The other is in the military, and his tour of duty takes him to the Persian Gulf as Operation Desert Storm heats up. Savannah's sister is married with two children, but she is not happy in the marriage, and, during the course of the novel, her husband loses his job. Despite their own disappointments in marriage, however, Savannah's sister and mother continually pressure her to get married. They remind her that at thirty-six, her opportunities to have children are running out.

At Gloria's birthday party, the four friends compare themselves to musical instruments. Savannah's best friend from college, Bernadine Harris, says she is like an upright bass because "they're always in the background but they carry the whole beat" (326). This comment accurately describes the function of Bernadine's story line in the novel. It is the only one of the four with a traditional conflict, crisis, and resolution.

Bernadine seemed to be living the American dream, but throughout the course of the novel, she is engaged in a struggle with her ex-husband, John. She helped him found a successful software company. They own a large house in an affluent suburb of Phoenix, a BMW, a Porsche, and a Jeep Cherokee. Their two children attend an exclusive private school. During their marriage, Bernadine frequently showed off her culinary skills entertaining John's business associates. Yet Bernadine had not been happy for years. Her husband convinced her to stay at home with the children until they reached school age, but Bernadine had wanted to start her own catering business. When she first appears in the novel, John has just announced he is divorcing her so that he can marry a white woman. In leaving Bernadine for a white woman, John has not only betrayed their marriage, he has also indicated that no black woman is good enough for him. Bernadine and her friends, as well as a large portion of McMillan's core black female audience, take John's defection as an assault on their honor. Bernadine's winning a just settlement, therefore, comes to symbolize all black women's desire for just treatment in the society at large.

When it is important for McMillan to present an eyewitness account of incidents that build the dramatic tension in Bernadine's story line, Bernadine serves as the viewpoint character. For example, McMillan gives readers direct access to Bernadine's thoughts and emotions when she hears from her children that their father got married and their new "mommy" is expecting a baby. Bernadine quips, "This is the best goddamn news I've heard all day" (334). Then she storms out of the room and locks herself in her bedroom. The developments in Bernadine's divorce are also the subject of reflection and discussion among other characters, even when Bernadine is not present. Gloria finds out about the divorce from Phillip, who works in her beauty shop. As they style customers' hair, he reveals, "John left her, honey. Get ready for this: for a white girl!" (73). In this way, Bernadine's story "carries the whole beat" and keeps readers interested in what happens next.

For Bernadine and her circle of friends, John's preference for a white woman is the ultimate betrayal. In a fit of rage, Bernadine dumps all of his designer clothes into his BMW and sets it on fire. Then she has a garage sale and sells the rest of his things, including his golf clubs, skis, and an antique car—all for only $1.00 per item. John's betrayal turns out to be even more devious, however, when Bernadine discovers he has closed their bank accounts and left her with no money to pay the mortgage.

Although she was an experienced bookkeeper, Bernadine had always let John handle all their financial affairs. Therefore, when her lawyer begins investigating discrepancies in John's financial statements, Bernadine is shocked to learn that he owned properties she knew nothing about. Worse, he has sold his share of the business to his partner at a price far below market value. John has been plotting so that when he filed for divorce, his income would appear much lower than it actually was. That way, he could reduce the amount of community property and child support he would have to pay Bernadine in the settlement. Throughout the novel, Bernadine struggles to cope with being "suddenly single" and to get a just settlement from John.

McMillan gives Bernadine a happy ending: a final settlement of almost $1 million—more than three times what John had initially offered. Bernadine's feminist divorce lawyer has put the fear of God and the IRS into John. Symbolically, Bernadine wins justice, often an elusive commodity in the lives of African American women. She also wins true love. As the novel closes, Bernadine is in a loving relationship with a civil rights attorney, James Wheeler, who has agreed to relocate to Phoenix to be with Bernadine. He also plans to fight to make the state honor the federal holiday on Martin Luther King, Jr.'s birthday. Thus, Bernadine's lover stands for justice. Further, the fact that his first wife was a white woman who died of breast cancer and that he has now chosen Bernadine restores the racial honor that John had besmirched at the start of the novel.

Though Bernadine enjoys a fairy-tale happy ending, McMillan had originally intended that Gloria Matthews would die. She had wanted to use Gloria's high blood pressure and obesity as an example of how health problems that are common in the black community frequently claim people well before their time. As the character developed, however, McMillan felt unable to kill her off. Gloria has been using food as her lover and coping mechanism for years. Thus, while she owns the most successful African American beauty salon in town and is universally recognized as a pretty woman, she wears a size 18 and weighs over two hundred pounds. Gloria is a single mother who has made her son, Tarik, the center of her life. But at seventeen, Tarik is beginning to assert his manhood. Gloria has not dated for years, but she has to cope with the knowledge that her son has become sexually active. Even more difficult for her is facing the fact that her son is almost ready to leave home. Letting Tarik go will require Gloria to define her own interests in life for the first time.

In the midst of these life adjustments, Gloria also gets caught up in a crisis at her shop. One of her stylists is a gay man who becomes sick with AIDS and has to stop working. Another of her stylists quits, and Gloria has a difficult time finding a skilled replacement. Chronically shorthanded, Gloria tries to cover more of the clients herself and ends up putting in twelve to fourteen-hour days. Then her poor health habits catch up with her, and she suffers a heart attack. With love and support from her family and friends, though, Gloria recovers and opens up to the possibility of a romance with her widowed neighbor.

The desire for justice and the search for a romantic partner are two of the motivations that drive the plot of *Waiting to Exhale*. Overall, however, the novel is about women's growth and personal development. Bernadine earns her happy ending because, after years of suppressing her own needs and desires in order to please John, the divorce motivates her to stand up for herself and fight for what she wants out of life. Gloria also grows enough to stop organizing her world around her son. In contrast, Bernadine's friend Robin does not learn much over the course of the novel. She has miserable luck with men, primarily because she makes such poor choices about whom to date. Robin places more value on physical attractiveness than on character. She has a bad habit of sleeping right away with the attractive men she dates instead of taking the time to get to know them first. Since she does not ask the right questions in the beginning of a relationship, she ends up involved with men who are committed to someone else or who have serious personal problems such as drug addiction.

Thus, McMillan leaves Robin pregnant with her lover Russell's child but disillusioned with Russell himself. Like Savannah, Robin tells her story in a first-person central voice that effectively engages readers. Robin, however, is a classic naive narrator, and McMillan deliberately manipulates the dramatic ironies of Robin's self-delusion to make a powerful comment on women who depend on men to validate their existence. Although Robin demonstrates competence in her work as an insurance underwriter, frequently arranging multimillion-dollar deals, her personal finances are a shambles. She has allowed her boyfriends to take advantage of her financially. She is also addicted to shopping for new clothes and sexy lingerie. Collection agents call her more frequently than the men she dates. Despite her foolish choices, Robin's friends appreciate her spontaneous, fun-loving personality. She is also a loyal, supportive friend. She helps Bernadine cope with the stress of her divorce by baby-sitting whenever Bernadine needs some time to herself. Robin

is also a devoted daughter caught up in the tragedy of her father's Alzheimer's disease. She drives to Tucson every other weekend to help her
mother care for her father. Unfortunately, she uses her familiar negative
patterns of undisciplined shopping and sexual addiction to escape from
these family problems. Further, while the other characters offer Robin
their friendship, they clearly disapprove of the choices she makes and
frequently lose patience with her willingness to let Russell and other men
take advantage of her.

NARRATIVE POINT OF VIEW

Orchestrating a narrative with multiple protagonists and story lines is
a complex task for a novelist. McMillan has further complicated this
technical challenge by alternating between first-person and third-person
narration. The easiest approach would have been to narrate the whole
novel in third-person shifting point of view, as she did in *Mama*. Yet,
despite McMillan's gift for using dialogue to create distinctive voices and
personalities for her characters, third-person narration would have made
it more difficult to differentiate among the characters. More specifically,
given that the four women are all around the same age and face similar
frustrations in their relationships with men, the task of evoking four
separate personalities would have been more difficult if McMillan had
relied exclusively on third-person narration.

A third-person narrator would also have distanced readers from the
characters, diminishing the sense of intimacy that makes *Waiting to Exhale* such a successful portrait of female friendship. By opening the novel
with Savannah's first-person confession about her difficulties finding a
husband, McMillan immediately draws the reader into the circle of
friends. Savannah confides in the reader as candidly as if she were talking to Bernadine, her best friend. Savannah's honesty enables her to see
and speak the truth about herself as well as about the other characters
in the book. She is, therefore, in a position to express judgments about
the other characters—judgments that might sound too preachy coming
from a third-person narrator. For example, after a session in the steam
room that concludes with a discussion of why Robin is afraid to be seen
eating in a restaurant by herself, Savannah looks at Robin's surgically
altered bosom and realizes that Robin is completely dependent on men
for her sense of self-esteem. She thinks to herself, "women who think
like her really piss me off" (203). A third-person narrator would not have

experienced any growth with that observation, but Savannah, who has always been self-conscious about her small breasts, does learn from the experience.

McMillan's decision to use first-person narration with Robin as well as Savannah makes Robin an even more effective foil. Savannah is constantly learning, growing, and sharing her insights throughout the novel. Robin continually repeats the same mistakes. First-person narration enables McMillan to make Robin's self-delusion perfectly clear to readers while allowing them to judge her for themselves. For example, by the time readers get to the chapter entitled "Closer to the Bone," they have heard Robin relate the whole saga of her relationship with Russell in four previous chapters devoted to her point of view. They know that Robin supported Russell financially for two years, hoping he would marry her. Instead, he took up with another woman. Readers have been privy to information that Russell has married and started a family but have watched Robin discount these facts as rumor.

When "Closer to the Bone" opens, Robin has allowed Russell to move back in with her. Readers wait with Robin while Russell is supposedly out asking his wife for a divorce. When he finally comes back to Robin, nothing is settled. At first, Robin is angry enough to confront him. When she smells his wife's perfume on the shirt he has dropped in the bathroom, she momentarily realizes Russell is not serious about a relationship with her. Then she immediately talks herself out of facing the truth: "Wait a minute! Hold it! Don't be so stupid, Robin. She was probably crying on his shoulder or something, being melodramatic. Begging him to come back. That's why his shirt smells like this" (311–12).

First-person central narration is effective for presenting Savannah and Robin, but juggling four first-person narrators would have been a great technical challenge. This choice would have required McMillan to fully differentiate among the four protagonists, relying almost exclusively on variations in their speech rhythms and word choices. In an interview with *Poets & Writers* magazine, McMillan explains that it would have taken too much effort to make this technique work when she preferred to keep the emphasis of the story on the women as a group. The three chapters in the novel that use third-person narration to bring the women together as a quartet of voices blend the characters and their story lines together very well. Overall, McMillan achieves an excellent balance by presenting Bernadine and Gloria as viewpoint characters in third-person narration, while Robin, the least self-aware character, and Savannah, the most perceptive, serve as foils for each other's first-person narration.

CHARACTER DEVELOPMENT

In choosing to structure her novel around four protagonists, McMillan might have developed characters who were widely divergent in appearance, socioeconomic status, and values. Doing so would have made distinguishing the characters a much easier task, but it would have been harder to convince readers they had enough in common to share such a rich friendship. Hence, Savannah, Bernadine, Robin, and Gloria are similar in many ways. They are all in their late thirties. Gloria, who turns thirty-eight during the novel, is the oldest. Robin, at thirty-five, is the youngest. Savannah and Bernadine are both thirty-six, going on thirty-seven for most of the book. Further, references to popular songs and current events such as the war in the Persian Gulf set the story in time around 1990. To be thirty-something at that moment in time is to be part of the baby boom—a generation that has grown up with a shared sense of identity defined by mass media and popular culture. When the friends gather at Gloria's house to celebrate her birthday, they tease her about not owning a CD player, but Gloria's album collection takes them back through earlier periods in their lives and through memories of the men with whom they shared those moments. These musical signifiers should trigger the same kinds of memories for readers who are part of the baby boom, enabling them to identify more closely with the characters. Whether the novel will remain as meaningful to readers who have never heard of Al Green and have no personal memories attached to "Let's Stay Together" is part of the larger question of the enduring significance of McMillan's work. Nevertheless, her use of such references to popular culture is one of her trademark techniques for evoking character and setting.

Savannah, Bernadine, Robin, and Gloria are also alike in that they are all members of the new black middle class. Desegregation has made it possible for them to complete college degrees and advance into well-paid professional positions in the white corporate world. Yet they are not free of money worries. Savannah supports her elderly mother. Robin would like to be able to help her mother pay for professional care for her father, who, as noted previously, is afflicted with Alzheimer's disease. Still, their clothes, home furnishings, and cars represent them as women of substance. Description of each woman's physical appearance and living space is, therefore, an important technique McMillan uses to present her characters. She demonstrates her skill by weaving these descriptions into interior monologue or dialogue between characters more often than she uses the third-person narrator to catalogue these details. Hence, we learn that Savannah has a small bosom but a shapely behind as she describes what she chooses to wear to a New Year's Eve party. We learn that Robin has breast implants when she advises Savannah to "buy you some," like she did. We learn that Bernadine has long hair when she muses about how she had to spend so much time taking care of it because John had threatened to leave if she ever cut it. Although the third-person narrator initially tells us that Gloria is about sixty pounds overweight, we learn that she is pretty when she remembers her son pleading, "you're too pretty to be fat."

Each woman's home also says a lot about her personality. Robin cherishes a collection of black dolls that represents her vulnerability and naivete, despite her extensive sexual experience. Gloria's home gives no indication that she majored in drama. Instead, it shows how thoroughly she has submerged her entire personality into her role as a mother. Her shop, however, is decorated in a "sort of funky chic" that expresses her dramatic flair. Bernadine's 4,000-square-foot Southwestern-style house in the suburbs is filled with material comforts and expensive artwork. It represents how much she had suppressed her own taste to please her husband. After he leaves, she realizes that there is nothing in the house that would indicate black people live there. Savannah's apartment, in contrast, is full of prints and sculptures by African American artists. Thus, McMillan skillfully uses setting to indicate significant differences among her characters even though they share similar socioeconomic circumstances. She uses action to differentiate them further.

Each woman has bad habits that betray her human imperfections. Gloria overeats. Savannah and Bernadine smoke. Robin is addicted to sex and shopping. Since Bernadine is the only character involved in a story line with a traditional conflict, McMillan uses more action to present her than the other characters. Bernadine's actions vividly express what she is feeling as she tries to cope with the divorce. She snatches the rollers out of her hair and throws them at John when he announces he is leaving. She burns up his clothes and sells his favorite things at a yard sale. When she finds out he has closed their bank accounts, she goes to his office, slaps her rival, and curses John. Then she remembers the checkbook for their American Express account and coolly writes herself a check for $16,000 to replace the money John took. Not all women would do such outrageous things, but Bernadine's actions express feelings with which anyone can identify. Further, the fact that she fights back so vigorously tells readers a lot about the kind of woman she is.

Appearance and action define the characters at a surface level, but since the women's personal growth and development is the underlying theme of the novel, the insights and emotions they reveal through interior monologue and dialogue are McMillan's most powerful tools for presenting them as distinct characters. For example, McMillan uses a rare passage of second-person central narration to illustrate Bernadine's dawning recognition that she had submerged her own personality over the course of her marriage. Beginning on page 30, Bernadine accuses herself: "Of course this is all your fault, Bernadine, because like a fool you acquiesced too soon and gave up too much." She then continues reviewing the history of her married life in a passage that portrays Bernadine as "beside herself" emotionally as she addresses herself as "you" (30–35). In addition, because she is the only one of the four friends who has ever been married, the failure of her marriage represents the failure of a common dream. Despite their strongest wishes and expectations, all four women find themselves facing the prospect of a life that may never include a male partner. As we have seen in the analysis of narrative voice, Savannah's observations provide the most powerful ironic commentary on this situation, while Robin's self-deception and palpably evident lack of self-esteem force readers as well as her circle of friends to examine their own choices.

Gloria appears to be the most passive of the four friends, but she also exemplifies the values they hold in common as she tries to transmit them to her son. When she discovers he has become sexually active, she has a frank conversation with him about birth control. As a young woman, she had considered herself a sinner for having premarital sex and conceiving a child out of wedlock. As a mother, however, she does not condemn Tarik's premarital sexual activity. Although she has not been as sexually active as her friends, she shares their open-mindedness. Similarly, when one of her gay employees falls sick with AIDS, she tries to provide him with financial assistance, and she speaks in his defense against bigots like her customer Sister Monroe. Savannah, Robin, and Bernadine all share Gloria's tolerant attitude toward homosexuality, even though men like Tarik's father might have made good husbands for them if it were not for their sexual orientation.

Gloria also wonders about the standards of beauty Tarik has internalized. He does not like "ugly" (meaning "fat") girls. When Gloria catches him with a white girlfriend, she wonders if she and other black women had done something wrong to cause their men to turn to white women. After this relationship ends and Tarik resumes dating black girls, Gloria observes, "For some reason, all the girls he brought home seemed to have the same thing in common: they all had long hair and light skin and were pretty" (295). Gloria's life may not be as eventful as her friends', but her thoughts reflect concerns she shares not only with them, but also with many of the readers. Thus, instead of creating four raging individualists, McMillan presents four friends who can be alter egos for her female readers.

While the appeal of *Waiting to Exhale* is not limited to female readers, the screen version of the story caused McMillan's name to become synonymous with male bashing. It is true that McMillan does not fully develop any of the male characters in the novel. The narrative never makes their thoughts accessible to the reader, so there are no psychological motivations to explain why the male characters do the things they do in the story. McMillan acknowledges that excluding the male point of view was a deliberate choice. She had already proved that she could develop a male character in his full human complexity with Franklin from *Disappearing Acts*. She wanted *Waiting to Exhale* to tell the women's story (Giles 38). What her detractors have rarely recognized is that the story explores why women make poor choices concerning the men in their lives.

Robin's boyfriends are despicable, but McMillan uses irony implicit in Robin's self-deluded narration to show that she is responsible for letting these men into her life and for continually allowing them to take advantage of her. The other three main characters regularly express their disapproval both of the men Robin dates and of Robin for chosing to date them. Similarly, Bernadine's husband treats her abominably, but McMillan uses the third-person omniscient narrator to express the judgment that Bernadine suffers, at least partly, because she had given up her power to John. She had allowed him to handle all their finances and had not bothered to keep informed about what they owned. The narrator comments, "Bernadine *had* trusted him all these years, and she had no idea how much it was going to cost her" (28). Bernadine's mother also remarks on how John "managed to turn you into this sappy woman while he did whatever in God's name he pleased" (139). She offers her support to her daughter but simultaneously implies that Bernadine should not have let John dominate her.

One advantage of having four protagonists in the novel is that readers can see how the characters perceive one another. Thus, it is possible for them to obtain a more rounded and well-balanced portrait of each protagonist. In this way, Gloria's abstinence from dating and her addiction to food as a replacement for love come under just as much scrutiny as Robin's pathetic relationships. Both Bernadine and Savannah are aware that Gloria has turned her son into a surrogate husband. A close reading of the novel therefore shows that McMillan turns the same critical light on her female protagonists that they themselves turn on the men in their lives.

LITERARY STYLE

The most remarkable element of McMillan's style is her ability to evoke an urban vernacular that black readers recognize as their own language. Savannah and Bernadine hail from Pittsburgh. Robin is a "military brat" whose father was stationed all over the world during her childhood. Although Gloria's parents were originally from Alabama, she was born and raised in Oakland, California. East Coast, West Coast, and rural southern black dialects have distinctive variations in pronunciation and vocabulary; yet, in terms of word choice and syntax, all four characters sound the same. But this is not a flaw in McMillan's technique. Rather, it is a sign that she is creating an artistic representation of vernacular black speech that allows her to engage her readership more effectively than absolutely authentic transcriptions of dialect would. As such, her style does not exclude readers from any ethnolinguistic background. Savannah's opening monologue on the book's first four pages reveals McMillan's ability to capture the rhetorical style of black English even while conforming to the rules of standard English grammar usage.

African American linguist Geneva Smitherman identifies four basic communicative modes in vernacular black English: call and response, signification, tonal semantics, and narrative sequencing. All four function within both secular and sacred contexts. As a blues testimonial, *Waiting to Exhale*, like McMillan's other novels, falls into the narrative sequencing, or storytelling, mode. Yet, within Savannah's monologue and throughout the novel, examples of the other three communicative modes also come into play.

To begin with, because the novel is a testimonial, it calls directly for some response from the reader, even though it is a print document. This is evident when McMillan reads from her work in public, as the audience "co-signs," or affirms what she is saying with the codified responses that are part of the traditional African American performance aesthetic: "Tell it," "Right on," and so forth. Savannah's first-person narrative voice speaks directly to the reader as if she is confiding in someone who can validate her experience. Additionally, McMillan builds significant pauses into her prose rhythm to create space for the reader to co-sign the experience. For example, the first paragraph of the novel uses complex discursive sentences to create a rhythm that climaxes in the shorter, aphoristic final sentence: "There's a big difference between being thirsty and being dehydrated" (1). The change in rhythm followed by the pause between paragraphs and the vivid metaphor, which is characteristic of African American rhetorical style, all combine to engage readers and move them to respond.

McMillan also incorporates instances of "signifying" into Savannah's monologue. "Signifying" is a complex mode of commenting, indirectly and usually unfavorably, about people and situations. Speakers of vernacular black English and literary critics such as Henry Louis Gates, Jr., who have analyzed the ways that African American writers use this rhetorical device commonly say that one "signifies *on*" something. The first sentence provides the clue that Savannah's entire monologue is an ironic commentary when she uses the phrase "all geeked up" to describe her attire for a formal New Year's Eve party. Originally, a "geek" was a carnival or sideshow entertainer who performed outlandish stunts such as biting the heads off live chickens. From this context, the term "geek" came to signify a "weird" person. According to Clarence Major's *Juba to Jive*, since the 1970s, "geek" has meant "an intellectual" in black slang. This connotation reflects the black community's distrust of those who value book learning over mother wit or lived experience. Savannah's use of the term signifies on the pretentiousness of the new black middle class by implying that this social scene is all an outlandish performance. The word "geek" itself is common in American slang, but the way Savannah uses it with additional connotative meaning instantly alerts readers familiar with vernacular black English that Savannah speaks their mother tongue.

Of the four communicative modes Smitherman identifies in black vernacular speech, tonal semantics is the most difficult to represent in print. Most of the African captives brought to the United States as slaves spoke tone languages in which pitch contours (high, low, rising, or falling) were semantically marked. Thus, a single syllable like "ba" could have many different meanings depending on how it was pronounced. African Americans have continued to use tone as a semantic marker in their speech even though English is not a tonal language. For example, African American speakers often shift vowels for emphasis: an "ooglay" person looks much worse than one who is merely ugly; a "partay" is a lot more fun than a party. Black speakers may also deviate from the standard accentual stress for similar reasons: the "*po*-lice" versus the "po-*lice*."

McMillan's decision not to employ alternative spelling makes it much harder for her to convey tonal semantics, but toward the end of Savannah's initial monologue, she uses italics to indicate tonal emphasis: "Of course she didn't bother asking this time. But Sheila did manage to remind me for the zillionth time that I'm running out of *time*" (4). It is no accident that the italicized word appears a total of three times in this sentence and the one preceding it, with the italics on only the third instance. Judicious repetition is a device that works well in all languages and literatures, but tonal semantics in vernacular black English allows speakers to add even more nuances of meaning to repeated elements, with subtle changes in pitch and stress for each occurrence. Thus, readers who are used to hearing pitch contours as semantic elements know exactly what Savannah sounds like as she mimics Sheila in indirect quotation, and they are attuned to both her surface and ironic meanings.

Mimicry is, in fact, another common element of vernacular black English tonal semantics. In this some monologue, when Savannah quotes her sister, Sheila, directly, members of black vernacular speech communities would expect her to shift into a voice that imitates Sheila's but mocks her at the same time. Of course, this kind of mockery is also a way of signifying on Sheila and her "happy housewife" lifestyle. While Savannah makes it very clear in this monologue that she is tired of being alone, her attitude toward Sheila betrays her ambivalence about marriage. Consequently, McMillan is simultaneously making effective use of black vernacular rhetorical style to develop Savannah's character: Is Savannah merely envious? Or does she express a valid critique of traditional marriage?

Savannah is one of four women who grapple with this question, but within her monologue, she tells several microstories to illustrate her opinion. This technique of using indirection and experiential rather than formal logic is a common feature of black vernacular narrative sequencing. In the first paragraph of the monologue, Savannah tells the story of how she got invited to the New Year's Eve party. Her mother and sister are concerned because she is not married, so her sister tries to fix her up with one of her husband's friends. In the next paragraph, Savannah tells stories about each of her family members. This strategy provides readers with a lot of information about Savannah's background and helps them get to know her. However, the stories also have a rhetorical function. One by one, Savannah shows that none of her family members is better off than she is; therefore, none is qualified to give her advice.

Savannah begins her attack with the common strategy of using a proverb to express conventional wisdom: "But Sheila and Mama have always thought that something was better than nothing" (1). Then she immediately signifies on this "wisdom" by adding, "and look where it's gotten them" (1). Savannah's father left seventeen years ago, but her mother is still bitter and brokenhearted. Her sister "files for divorce on an annual basis" (1). One of her brothers is in jail for pulling a stupid stunt, and the other one is "a lifer in the Marine Corps" (2). This last turn of phrase is also a masterful piece of signifying, because "lifer" originally meant a convict serving a life sentence in prison. In Savannah's mind, then, this brother is just as stupid as the one who is actually in jail for passing counterfeit money.

Since Savannah's opening comment about being "all geeked up" has established lived experience as the basis of the authority with which she speaks, her dismissal of her family's lived experiences also discounts them as credible authorities: "So far as taking advice from *any* of them goes, I'm skeptical" (2). Here again, italics evoke Savannah's tonal semantics. At the same time, in the context of the vernacular language she has used up to this point, the word "skeptical" becomes a rhetorical flourish that Smitherman identifies as "high talk." An even more effective instance of high talk occurs in the next paragraph, when Savannah juxtaposes "inconsequential" with "shit": "For the last three years my life has felt inconsequential, like nobody really gives a shit what I'm doing or how well I do it" (2).

McMillan's propensity for using profanity has offended some readers and reviewers, but within the black vernacular speech community, the four-letter words and variations on them frequently function as grammatical intensifiers that can emphasize either good or bad meanings. McMillan makes such use of "ass" in the very first paragraph of the book, when Savannah explains that Sheila's "simple-ass husband" is a friend of the man who invited her to the party. The "good old Anglo-Saxon" terms are part of general American parlance, but constructions such as "simple-ass" derive from black vernacular slang and rhetorical styles. There are other terms McMillan could use that speakers of black English would readily recognize but that readers outside that speech community would not. Part of McMillan's stylistic genius, then, is to take common slang terms like "hunky-dory" and use them with a specifically African American flair.

For example, when Savannah explains how, after the annual breakup of Sheila's marriage, Sheila stops calling except to give "a three-minute synopsis of how hunky-dory everything is now," her use of mainstream slang signifies on how fake Sheila's life is. In fact, Clarence Major notes, " 'Hunky-dory' is not of black origin but is popular among black slang users, especially when improvised" (246). He cites McMillan's essay "The Love We've Lost" as the definitive example of such improvisation: "We parade around as if life is so hunky-fuckin-dory, but it's so phony, and the energy it takes to fake it begins to wane" (McMillan 1993, 78). This kind of improvisational combination is a common feature of African American style, whether in music, fashion, or speech. Hence, McMillan's manipulation of standard English continually celebrates an African American worldview, even though her work appears to not directly protest the political and economic constraints racism imposes on African Americans.

In fact, in the course of Savannah's monologue, Sheila makes reference to these very realities, questioning Savannah's decision to move to Arizona, "where that governor rescinded the King holiday after it had already been passed" (12). Savannah reminds her sister that her best friend lives in Arizona and tells another microstory about driving sixty miles in a snowstorm to be a bridesmaid in Bernadine's wedding as a testimony of how strong this friendship is. She then uses proverbial statement once again to remind Sheila that Bernadine has "been black all her life." Her response to the King holiday issue is that she will be the first one in line at the polls.

Savannah's language reflects a worldview and a philosophy of living that are consonant with the blues aesthetic. The blues testimonial form does not require the performer to solve problems. Rather, the function of the blues testimonial is to acknowledge problems. Further, in Savannah's eyes, the experiential logic of her bond with Bernadine is more compelling than the formal logic of assuming that Arizona is an impossible place for blacks to live. When Savannah concludes her monologue with the proverbial declaration that Sheila "gets on my last nerve," African American readers familiar with this expression can fully co-sign her testimony. Meanwhile, McMillan's decision to use standard English grammar and vocabulary makes it possible for readers of any ethnolinguistic background to affirm the experience.

THEMATIC ISSUES: A GOOD MAN IS HARD TO FIND

Waiting to Exhale turns on the reality that there are more women than men in the world, as well as on the female perception that there is a shortage of eligible men, particularly in the African American community. In the United States, women born in the first ten years of the baby boom, between 1946 and 1957, have been at a disadvantage in finding mates because women are expected to marry a man the same age as or slightly older than themselves. Since few children were born during the depression and war years (1929–1945), the women born in the first years of the baby boom far outnumber the men born ahead of them, who normally would have provided their pool of eligible husbands. Moreover, because men often marry women who are considerably younger than they are, the women born early in the baby boom have not only had to compete with one another for the eligible men in their age range, but they have also had to face competition from the vast number of younger women in the boomer generation. McMillan brings such bald statistics to life: in *Waiting to Exhale*, not only is Bernadine's rival white, she is also a good ten years younger.

At the same time, McMillan demonstrates how the experience of women born in the early years of the baby boom has redefined the role of women in American society. In the 1950s, little girls expected to grow up, marry, and raise children like their mothers. However, increased affluence made it possible for more of those little girls to attend college or seek other kinds of professional training. Women were freer to pursue careers than ever before. Women born early in the baby boom led the way for women to participate actively in almost all sectors of the American economy and in almost all facets of Americans institutions. Still, at every step of the way, they were haunted by traditional expectations that they should be at home raising children full-time. McMillan's Savannah therefore discovers that professional success and the ability to support her mother count for nothing in the eyes of her family because she has not married. Savannah herself feels that something is wrong because she has failed to find a husband and start a family. The *Cosmopolitan* girl's goal of having it all—marriage, children, and career—has proved a difficult balancing act for women like Savannah and her friends.

As the boomers came of age and attempted to start families, the divorce rate skyrocketed, so that many of the women who had defined their lives in terms of traditional roles found themselves raising children alone, struggling to compete successfully in the workforce, and searching for a new partner with whom they could form a permanent union. Hence, in McMillan's tale, although Bernadine originally dreamed of running a catering business, she acquiesced to her husband's desire for a traditional stay-at-home wife only to be cast aside after eleven years of marriage.

Yet McMillan's characterizations also dramatize changing mores that offered women of the baby boom unprecedented freedom to define their own sexuality. The invention of the birth control pill and the legalization of abortion were two landmark events that contributed to a climate of changing social mores known as the "sexual revolution" of the 1960s and 1970s. The women of *Waiting to Exhale*, like many women of their generation, regard the search for sexual fulfillment as a valid human endeavor. Indeed, McMillan demonstrates her awareness that her audience shares this attitude when she allows Savannah to provide a comic description of a lover who growls like a bear during the sex act. Earlier generations of women readers might have judged Savannah negatively as a "loose woman" instead of applauding her frank acknowledgment of what a woman does and does not look for in a lover. Thus, *Waiting to Exhale* struck a chord similar to that of other forms of popular women's fiction, such as romance novels, which also invite women readers into a dialogue about new roles women can play in intimate relationships.

Women readers consider this dialogue to be vitally important because changing mores have radically altered the way that men and women try to relate to each other in romantic partnerships. Both sexes had grown up with one set of expectations about gender roles, but both have been in the process of redefining those expectations. Since individuals often have conflicting ideas about appropriate gender behavior even within themselves, it is small wonder that men and women often find themselves in intense conflict about how they should behave toward each other. Women look to popular fiction, women's magazines, self-help books, and television talk shows for advice and support in their efforts to redefine themselves and their relationships with men.

For African American women, the tensions created by changing gender roles have been exacerbated by a significant disparity in sex ratios— on average, there are only 83 black men for every 100 black women. In some urban areas, this sex differential is even greater. McMillan draws on this reality to portray frustrations with which her core audience of African American women can readily identify. During the 1980s, many young professional black women like Savannah discovered too late that leaving their hometown communities and moving to advance their careers had greatly decreased their chances of finding an eligible black male partner. "The deal is, the men are dead in Denver" Savannah quips (2). But they were also literally and figuratively dead in Detroit, D.C., and in Dallas.

Various factors contribute to the inordinately high mortality rate of African American men. In addition to decreased access to medical care and the impact of violent crime, the Vietnam War also took a toll on the pool of black men who might have been eligible mates for black women in Savannah's generation. During the early years of the war, African Americans constituted only 11 percent of the U.S. population, but black servicemen made up 23 percent of the casualties (Wallace xv–xvi). In fact, Savannah remembers that the boyfriend she probably should have married went to Vietnam.

McMillan also explores the changing definition of what constitutes an "eligible man" in the eyes of upwardly mobile African American women. For most, this means a man from a similar socioeconomic background. In other words, an eligible man should have at least as much education as the woman, should earn at least as much but preferably more money than she does, and should be somewhat older than she is. African American women born during the first cohort of the baby boom started out facing a demographic disadvantage that was magnified by these expectations.

Throughout the 1970s and 1980s, black women earned more college degrees than black men. For example, in 1992, the year *Waiting to Exhale* appeared, black women constituted 10.8 percent of female students enrolled in college while black men were only 8.2 percent of the male student population (Smith and Horton 199–200). The more education an African American woman obtained, the less likely she was to find a male with a comparable level of educational attainment. McMillan creates female characters who personalize these statistics by translating them into human terms. In the same way, McMillan makes the economic circumstances of her time understandable as forces that have a tangible impact on the lives of her characters. Her pairing of college-educated Zora with blue-collar Franklin in *Disappearing Acts* illustrates how the economic uncertainties of the 1980s made it difficult for black men to make up in earning power what they did not have in terms of educational attainment, a compensation that would make them eligible mates for upwardly mobile black women.

Although McMillan does not dwell on harsh statistics such as the disproportionate number of African American men in prison, the fictional worlds she creates do not gloss over such realities either. In *Mama*, Money, the only male in the Peacock brood, bounces in and out of prison for years before he kicks his heroin addiction. When *Waiting to Exhale* opens, Savannah's brother is doing time for passing counterfeit money. In 1993, the year after the novel appeared, black men made up 44.1 percent of the state and federal prison population (Smith and Horton 117). Thus, McMillan's representation of black male incarceration as a fact that touches the families of even the most ambitious African American women rings true to life.

Normally, a prison record would disqualify a man from the "eligible" standard. Yet, with so few men to choose from, publications targeting African American women, like *Essence* magazine, frequently ran articles on "the black man shortage" throughout the 1980s and advised their upwardly mobile readers to change their expectations of what constituted an acceptable mate. Among the solutions proposed was "man sharing," or a revival of African polygynous marriage, but most often, readers were urged to consider working-class men who made less money and had less education than they did. In that decade, black women novelists, including Alice Walker and Gloria Naylor, also flirted with representations of lesbian relationships as a fulfilling alternative to heterosexual marriage. Nevertheless, many other African American women condemned black gay men for further reducing their pool of eligible partners. In *Waiting to Exhale*, McMillan applies her deft humorous touch to this volatile subject in the scene where the father of Gloria's son announces that he is gay. Gloria, who had been hoping to entice David into her bed for old times' sake, protests that this is just a ruse to avoid spending the night with her.

Even more than by the loss of potential spouses due to homosexuality or imprisonment, many black women have been deeply hurt by the fact that an increasing number of black men choose to marry outside the race, another real-life heartache that McMillan acknowledges. By analyzing data on interracial marriage in the 1990 natural census, University of Michigan researchers found that "8% of black men between 25 and 34 years old were married to someone outside their race" ("Interracial Marriages Rising" 16). These men would have been considered too young for Savannah, Bernadine, Gloria, and Robin, all in their late thirties, but McMillan taps into the pain and anger interracial marriage provokes for many black women when she portrays Bernadine's husband leaving her to marry a white woman.

The blockbuster success of *Waiting to Exhale* reflects the fact that the institution of marriage is undergoing a major transformation in the black community. The African American divorce rate is more than twice the divorce rate for whites—263 per 1,000 compared to 124 per 1,000, respectively (Saluter 3). Given the impact of racism and economic discrimination on black male/black female romantic partnerships, these figures are not surprising. Criticism that McMillan's work does not address racial issues ignores the context out of which her fiction grows. Such criticism also denies McMillan's skill in representing political and economic problems, not as abstract principles, but as realities that affect intimate relationships in the lives of her characters in the same way that they affect intimate relationships in the lives of her readers.

Waiting to Exhale is, in fact, a significant contribution to a larger dialogue within the African American women's imagined print community about the dire shortage of eligible African American men. Overall, the cultural nationalist values of this imagined print community seek to preserve racial and ethnic identity. Thus, while definitions of "eligible" may be revised to include men of lower socioeconomic status or even men who have a primary attachment to another woman, seeking a mate outside the African American community is a less popular solution. The Michigan study reflects the fact that marrying outside the race, especially marrying white men, has remained a strong taboo for African American women, despite the shortage of African American men: only 4 percent of African American women aged twenty-five to thirty-four were married to someone of another race in 1990 ("Interracial Marriages Rising" 16). Indeed, African American romance novels show a strong nativist bent and rarely depict black heroes from Africa or the Caribbean, let alone from other racial or ethnic backgrounds. Nevertheless, the ongoing dialogue within the imagined print community fosters a process through which a generation of women are redefining themselves. McMillan's next novel successfully counters this nativist definition of an eligible man. In *How Stella Got Her Groove Back*, McMillan departs from her earlier social realism and creates for her African American heroine a happily-ever-after romance with a Jamaican man. The novel and its film adaptation have sparked a new trend in Caribbean tourism as sisters flock to the tropics to "get their groove back."

McMillan's novels, therefore, like popular women's fiction in general, provide readers with a forum for considering the ramifications of problems that women face in the most important aspect of their daily lives—their relationships with friends, family, and lovers. If nothing else, the trials of Savannah, Bernadine, Robin, and Gloria reassure black women that they are not alone and that their singleness is not a sign of personal failure. Since similar demographic forces have transformed women's roles throughout American society, McMillan can simultaneously appeal to a broad spectrum of female readers who have experienced similar frustrations in their personal relationships.

ALTERNATIVE INTERPRETATION: FORMALIST READING OF THE FOUR-WOMAN NOVEL

Formalist criticism emphasizes close interpretive reading of texts without reference to "external" factors such as the author's psychology or the social history of the period in which the text was written. The preceding analysis of plot development, narrative point of view, characterization, and language and diction in *Waiting to Exhale* constitutes a traditional formalist study of the structural elements McMillan employs. The above exploration of theme, however, departs from formalist analysis because it does refer to factors outside the text. Feminist critics have often found the traditional formalist approach inadequate for assessing the works of women writers because the aesthetic standards established by male critics did not take women's experience into account. Since women most often wrote about the domestic spaces that they knew rather than the broader social arenas that were the province of men, academic critics dismissed the themes women addressed (such as the age-old problem of finding a suitable husband) as insufficiently representative of "universal" human experience.

Not only has women's fiction differed in its thematic concerns, women writers have also used more noncanonical forms, or forms that fall beyond those of the established classical texts, to represent their experience. Since women's educational opportunities were long limited, women writers did not often have the training necessary to produce classical forms such as the long epic poem or the five-act drama. Critics have often dismissed forms women writers have frequently used (diaries, letters, and romance novels among them) as non literary. Consequently, one of the preoccupations of feminist critics and writers has been to identify and increase the status of forms that constitute a distinct women's literary tradition. In *Waiting to Exhale*, McMillan exhibits exceptional artistry through her structural and thematic manipulation of a classic form in American women's fiction—the four-woman novel.

A staple of American popular fiction since Louisa May Alcott developed it in *Little Women*, the four-woman form evolved organically out of Alcott's experience growing up in a close-knit family of four girls. Like Alcott, McMillan also grew up with three sisters and is therefore able to realistically represent the emotional bonds that can hold diverse groups of women together. The four-woman novel's rich potential for portraying female friendship accounts for the tremendous commercial success the genre has enjoyed. From *Little Women* to Rona Jaffe's *The Best of Everything* and more recent offerings such as Amy Tan's *The Joy Luck Club* to Julia Alvarez's *How the Garcia Girls Lost Their Accents*, the four woman-novel is an important fixture in American women's literary history.

Critics are still debating the literary merits of *Little Women*, but no one can deny its popular appeal. It has been a beloved favorite of American girls since its initial publication in 1868. Unfortunately, the tendency to make rigid distinctions between high culture and popular culture is one factor that has prejudiced critics against *Little Women* and other forms of popular fiction written by and for women. Traditionally, literary critics have assumed that writing with the objective of making money somehow taints the artistic purity of a work. Thus, the fact that Alcott wrote *Little Women* on contract, expanded the book at the urgent behest of her publisher and readers, and ultimately made a career of writing "girl books" because they paid the bills has added to the tendency to dismiss her work as sentimental fluff. Romance novels are disdained for similar reasons. They are written by and for women, and it is assumed that the authors are inspired more by the profit motive than by the desire to express an artistic vision. Even when a book is well crafted, commercial success can make the literary establishment question its artistic value. There is a lingering bias that real art cannot be accessible to the mass audience. Hence, McMillan herself expected that critics would attack *How Stella Got Her Groove Back*, if only because her previous novel, *Waiting to Exhale*, had been such a tremendous commercial success.

While the four-woman form emerged naturally from Alcott's autobiographical experience, she pioneered the simultaneous development of four female protagonists as a strategy for presenting a feminist message about the shared challenges all women face in male-dominated society. Alcott's nineteenth-century text relies on a third-person omniscient narrator who can see into the innermost thoughts of every character in the book. McMillan, who had experimented with dual protagonists in her earlier works, builds on Alcott's model for managing multiple protagonists by blending the intimacy of first-person narration with the collective experience Alcott had presented in the third person. As a result, McMillan's narrative immediately invites readers to participate in the sisterhood presented in the text and in the larger imagined community shared by readers who know and love the conventions of the four-woman novel. Readers recognize this narrative space as a forum for exploring the evolving facets of female identity in society.

First and foremost of the roles the four-woman novel has invited readers to consider is that of woman as artist. *Little Women* has been of particular significance in the lives of American girls who aspired to be writers. While Alcott used a third-person omniscient narrator to present the lives and inner thoughts of the four March sisters, Jo is the most fully drawn character in the book, and readers tend to identify most strongly with her tomboy rebellion against the feminine role. For the young author, Jo is also an important role model because the novel chronicles her struggle to succeed as a professional writer. Jo is the character closest to Alcott herself, so that *Little Women* provides young girls with both fictional and real-life examples of women pursuing literary careers.

Indeed, as a teenager, McMillan identified with Alcott's determination to earn money to support her parents and sisters because she herself was shelving books in the public library to earn money for the family kitty when she discovered a biography of this pioneering woman writer. At the time, McMillan did not envision a literary career for herself, but her success has in turn inspired a whole school of younger writers who regularly invoke *Waiting to Exhale* as a touchstone in the fictional worlds their characters inhabit. McMillan's phenomenal best-seller therefore has clear antecedents in an American women's literary tradition and exhibits a strong influence on the continuing evolution of American women's fiction. Having established the parameters of McMillan's chosen form, it is now possible to make a formalist evaluation of her text.

The four-woman novel is a character-driven form. Through the four main characters, the author can present a multiplicity of perspectives while emphasizing the commonality of experience women share across race, class, or cultural backgrounds in male-dominated society. Consequently, the four-woman form enables authors to reach a broad audience. If a woman does not see herself in the book, she probably knows someone who is like one of the characters. Even men may recognize aspects of women they know in the characters. In order to realize the strengths of this form, the author must be able to create engaging characters who are believable not only as individuals, but also in their intimate relationships with the other characters. *Waiting to Exhale* succeeds because McMillan skillfully creates a group of characters that a broad spectrum of readers can embrace as intimate friends.

Savannah, Bernadine, Robin, and Gloria have very different experiences when it comes to the one traditional constant of women's identity—their relationships with men. Only Bernadine has been a traditional housewife. Gloria, like Bernadine, is a mother, but she has never been married. And both Savannah and Robin are beginning to fear that they may never marry or establish their own families. McMillan's characterization techniques draw these four women together not only in the three chapters of the novel where third-person narrative presents their voices in concert, but all through the text. The women talk to one another. They think about one another even when they are not in one another's presence. They do things together, and they do things for one another. Thus, although they hail from different parts of the country and are pursuing very different careers, McMillan convincingly depicts their commonality of experience and outlook as members of an emerging black middle class.

The importance of sisterhood as an emotional support base that can sustain women through the activist efforts necessary to manifest their value in the world has always been a feature of the four-woman novel. *Little Women* is set during the Civil War era. With their father off at the front, each of the four March sisters must work at improving herself and her corner of the world. Alcott conceived of the novel as a female version of *Pilgrim's Progress*, John Bunyan's seventeenth-century allegory of the Christian soul's path to salvation. Her legacy therefore makes the four-woman novel a chronicle of women's spiritual development. McMillan is working within a blues cosmology rather than the traditional Christian system of morality, but her four protagonists all belong to an organization that exemplifies the reformist goals spiritual feminism has championed since the nineteenth century.

McMillan cannot resist satirizing the human foibles of the members attending a Black Women on the Move meeting. Nevertheless, her characters sincerely endorse the organization's programs, which support a scholarship fund, a prenatal care clinic, and community service projects targeting the elderly and the homeless. The group also sponsors workshops that provide the African American community with information on managing personal finances, starting a business, single parenting, coping with drug abuse in the family, and other mental health issues.

Nineteenth century feminist reformers would have looked for spiritual rather than psychodynamic sources of healing "Stress and Depression in the Black Female," but writers like Frances E. W. Harper who was active in the Women's Christian Temperance Movement (WTCU) and Ida B. Wells who worked with the National Association of Colored Women would have approved BWTOM's agenda. Despite the conflicts these nineteenth century black feminists sometimes had with white women in the women's suffrage movement, real-life counterparts of the fictional March sisters also saw their own spiritual development as intricately bound up with programs of reform work carried out in communities of women. McMillan's *Waiting to Exhale* enjoyed tremendous popular success because it spoke to the frustration a whole generation of women felt in their efforts to find a good man. Yet the book has come to occupy an important place in many women's spiritual lives because the real story is about Savannah's, Bernadine's, Robin's, and Gloria's spiritual growth. McMillan's artistry is therefore most evident in her ability to give a blues testimonial inflection to the classic spiritual concerns of the four-woman form.

In fact, McMillan exploits the fundamental flexibility of the four-woman novel to represent African American women's experience, just as Alcott originally developed the form as an expression of an American rather than a British literary sensibility. Alcott consciously modified models from British women's literature such as Jane Austen's *Pride and Prejudice*, which features five rather than four sisters, in order to define American female identity. She deliberately incorporated New England regionalisms into the March sisters' speech, just as McMillan creates an African American vernacular prose style in order to express African American identity.

Other critics have attacked McMillan for allegedly downplaying racial tensions in an effort to attract a crossover audience. Yet these critics have not understood the reformist politics of the four-woman form and the strategies it uses to address social issues important to women across race, class, and culture. The four-woman form can be ideal for raising such issues because it gives the author an opportunity to explore how different women respond to similar circumstances and because it allows the author and her audience to try out a variety of different solutions to common problems. For McMillan and her core audience, the ability to imagine a world in which being black and female is not an issue is an empowering act. Within the imagined community that McMillan and her readers share, black women exist as autonomous subjects. If the assumption that a black female perspective can be a valid way of looking at the world does not match black women's lived reality, the ability to imagine and act as if it is so sustains black women in their ongoing effort to make their reality part of the larger American landscape. McMillan continues this strategy of manipulating the forms of popular women's fiction to foreground black female experience in her next novel, *How Stella Got Her Groove Back*.

6

How Stella Got Her Groove Back
(1996)

How Stella Got Her Groove Back is most widely known for the "scandalous" older woman/younger man romance it presents. Yet what really puts Stella back "in the groove" is her reconnection with her own artistic desire. In fact, McMillan uses the blues romance pairing between a world-weary black woman and a "trifling" black man to make her love story a symbol of black female artistic development. As in Zora Neale Hurston's classic blues romance, *Their Eyes Were Watching God*, McMillan's Stella finds fulfillment in the creative process of narrating her experience rather than in the procreative process of bearing her lover's child. Moreover, the older woman/younger man romance challenges the foundations of patriarchal, male-dominated marriage by separating female sexuality from reproduction. Thus, McMillan skillfully manipulates the forms of popular romance to explore and question traditional expectations of women's roles. In a significant departure from her earlier social realism, McMillan adapts the idealized happily-ever-after ending from popular romance to fit the perspective of African American blues romance, offering a testimonial on the transformative power of love in the process.

PLOT DEVELOPMENT

All of McMillan's novels challenge stereotypes about black life. By representing affectionate bonds within the black community, she exposes the contradictions inherent in the images of blacks that have pervaded the popular American imagination for centuries. Her fiction humanizes African Americans by demonstrating that they love one another in a complex variety of roles, including parent and child, romantic lovers, and "sistah" friends. Until her fourth novel, McMillan had consistently chosen to represent these loving relationships in the context of the often harsh realities that blacks experience due to the social and economic pressures of institutional racism. *How Stella Got Her Groove Back* is an important departure from this social realism, for although the novel ostensibly parallels the author's own experience of fantastical material wealth and romance with a younger man, McMillan provides the story with a happily-ever-after ending that situates it more properly in the idealized realm of popular romance. At the same time, McMillan uses the shocking older woman/younger man love story to critique the escapist vision of love popular romance offers its readers.

McMillan attacks this escapist vision of love on several fronts. First of all, throughout the novel, Stella expresses criticism of the happily-ever-after fantasy of marriage that popular romance propagates. One of Stella's earliest comments is that her sister Angela sees marriage as the end of the rainbow, while she had wanted it to *be* the rainbow. Popular romance usually does portray marriage as the end of the rainbow. Although many romance novels rely on the "marriage of convenience plot," and reuniting divorced couples is almost a subgenre in itself, popular romance rarely depicts how husbands and wives live together after they have pledged their love and reached a mutual understanding.

McMillan's decision to focus on an unconventional older woman/younger man romance also serves as a powerful criticism of the institutional controls patriarchal marriage has traditionally imposed on female sexuality. Since women's childbearing years are limited, a younger wife is of more value than one whose biological clock is about to wind down. A young man like Winston paired with an older woman like Stella might forfeit the opportunity to father children of his body by remaining monogamously attached to her. This kind of union necessarily separates sexuality from procreation, an ideological shift which popular romance does not endorse. Consequently, McMillan's manipulation of popular romance conventions radically subverts the maternal imperative which is an integral component of the standard happy ending.

Above all, popular romance re-affirms family. Children are part and parcel of the happily-ever-after ending. Whether she has her own children, is gallantly raising orphaned children, adopts the hero's children, or experiences a delayed motherhood after finding the long-awaited man of her dreams, the romance heroine is almost never excused from maternity.

For this reason, older women who are nearing the end of their child-bearing years have only recently begun to appear as heroines in popular romance novels. Middle-aged baby boomers of Stella's generation have delayed maternity to the edge of biological limits but the over forty heroine jeopardizes the conventional "baby makes three" happy ending. Stella, a well-toned, youthful forty-two, who has already produced one healthy child, could easily produce several more children. Yet her response to the idea of bearing another child is resoundingly negative: "I do not would not dream of could not even fathom changing another pissy poopy Pamper or getting up in the middle of the night to a screaming I-need-a-bottle baby" (138). Instead, McMillan draws on the blues romance tradition established by Zora Neale Hurston in *Their Eyes Were Watching God* and emphasizes the fulfillment Stella finds in inventing her own life rather than expounding the maternal joys of nurturing new life.

Thus, *How Stella Got Her Groove Back*, the story of a forty-two-year-old woman trying to re-define her life, is the first of McMillan's novels to focus on a single protagonist. When the novel opens, Stella has just sent her son to visit his father (her ex-husband) for two weeks. Having taken vacation time from her job, Stella contemplates a number of projects and recreational activities (from planting more flowers in her yard to catching up on some pleasure reading) that she might pursue while her son is away. Stella has recently lost her best friend to liver cancer, but even before this tragedy, she had been feeling depressed and lethargic. Lack of a romantic partner was only one of the empty spaces in her life.

As is typical of McMillan's work, however, the plot does not follow a traditional conflict-crisis-resolution structure. The central conflict in the novel is one in which Stella struggles to overcome her doubts and fears. One of her statements sums up the crux of her romantic dilemma very well: "What I do know deep down although I keep it secretly secret is that I am terrified at the thought of losing myself again wholeheartedly to any man" (93). Thus, Stella is struggling with the issues of trust that romance writers very often use as the basis of the central conflict in a love story.

By chance, Stella sees an advertisement promoting Jamaican tourism on television and decides to visit the island. She rushes to her travel agent to book a ten-day stay in an adults-only resort. Then she goes on a shopping spree for new bathing suits and beachwear. Stella's sister Angela disapproves of this spur-of-the-moment adventure. Angela, married and pregnant with twins, has always championed the traditional, stay-at-home wife role. Stella's other sister, Vanessa, believes it will be good for Stella to do something spontaneous, and she agrees to water Stella's plants and feed her pets while she is gone. She also wants to borrow money from Stella.

Stella's parents started out in the projects in Chicago, but they were able to move to a house in the suburbs and send their children to well-appointed public schools. Stella, the oldest child, has most fully realized her family's upwardly mobile aspirations. She has an M.B.A., and she works as a securities analyst earning over $250,000 a year. She also has a strong portfolio of investments, which enables her to maintain a very comfortable lifestyle. She owns a large suburban home, a BMW, and a sporty truck. She can easily afford to fly to Jamaica first-class on a whim.

In Negril, Stella enjoys running along the beach every morning. She joins in volleyball games and goes horseback riding in the mountains, where she is dazzled by the natural beauty of the island. She also meets a friendly Canadian couple who are on their honeymoon, an older black man who keeps trying to talk her into sunbathing on the nude beach; and two African American women from Chicago who become her confidantes. When Stella attracts a younger Jamaican man, however, she does not know what to do.

Stella finds Winston Shakespeare irresistible. Not only is he is tall, lean, and sexy, he smells delicious. They enjoy each other's company and share many laughs. Still, she cannot understand why a twenty-one-year-old man would be interested in a woman twice his age. All through the novel, Stella struggles with her reservations about Winston's age. However, his attitude is very mature, and he touches her heart. Their mutual attraction is more than just lust.

On the flight back to California, Stella reads an article about vacation "flings." Hard as she tries, she cannot stop thinking about Winston. Once home, Vanessa notices that she looks refreshed and is glad that Stella got to enjoy some attention from the opposite sex. Angela, on the other hand, is scandalized by the affair. She warns Stella that Winston is probably out to take advantage of her because she has money. Angela's recriminations echo Stella's own fears, but in her heart, she feels that the experience was more than just a fling. She and Winston exchange postcards. Then they begin calling each other. Finally, when Stella's son says he wants to see Jamaica, she books another trip to the island. Since Winston has to work during most of her visit, he and Stella do not get to see much of each other. However, Stella's son likes Winston. Young Quincy exuberantly leads his mother into new adventures like cliff diving. By the time Stella has to return, she knows that the relationship with Winston could be serious.

Many popular romance stories feature emotionally detached heroes who are afraid to expose their vulnerabilities. Heroines who have been burned by love before and are wary of trusting another man are also quite common. In addition, romance heroes and heroines are frequently afraid to trust themselves. They may doubt their own ability to choose a partner who has their best interests at heart. They may lack confidence in their ability to attract and hold the interest of a loving partner. They may also be tormented by a sense of unworthiness and believe they do not deserve to be happy and loved. Stella exhibits all these fears, and readers can universally identify with her feelings.

Back home, however, Stella has many other decisions to make about the direction of her life. Her employer suddenly fires her. Fortunately, Stella has enough savings and investments to last for two or three years. Ironically, losing her job makes her realize that she did not enjoy working as a securities analyst anyway. In addition to her master's in business, she also has an master's of fine arts degree. Before she got caught up on the corporate treadmill, she had enjoyed creating "functional sculpture" and "wearable art." Stella decides that she does not want to work in the corporate world any longer. Predictably, Angela thinks this decision is foolish, while Vanessa supports it. Stella realizes that the time has come for her to take more risks in life, so she sends Winston a first-class ticket to California.

It takes several months for Winston to get time off from his job so that he can come visit Stella. She has many doubts during this period, but she also spends this time learning to relax and bond more closely with her son. When Winston finally does arrive, Stella also has a panic reaction to the idea of sharing her space with another person. Emptying drawers, making space in the closet, and clearing her toiletries off the countertop in the bathroom have powerful symbolic meaning for her.

Fortunately, Stella and Winston are able to talk through their fears with each other. Angela meets Winston and finally accepts him when she sees that he makes Stella happy. By the end of the novel, Stella has learned that she is entitled to be happy. When Winston asks her to marry him, she overcomes her doubts and reaches for a happily-ever-after ending.

While Stella's dilemma is one that all readers can potentially relate to, many reviewers have commented that the plot is not well developed. McMillan herself has acknowledged that she had to restructure the story for the screenplay in order to add more dramatic tension. Yet, as always, her novel's form follows a well-defined artistic vision. McMillan demonstrates clear understanding of the devices successful romance writers use to develop their plots. For example, on Stella's second visit to Jamaica, her phone is out of order for three days. She becomes anxious because there are no messages from Winston. Not knowing that the phone is broken, she thinks that Winston is rejecting her. In a typical romance novel, authors use many more mix-ups and misunderstandings of this kind to dramatize and intensify the emotions. McMillan could have used the geographical distance between Winston and Stella to add more powerful obstacles and make the story more plot driven. Instead, her interest is in the psychological drama that takes place inside Stella's head.

NARRATIVE POINT OF VIEW

McMillan employs many aspects of the popular romance genre in *How Stella Got Her Groove Back*, but she also stretches the form to fit her own artistic vision. Popular romance writers rarely use first-person central narration, but McMillan does so in this novel. One difficulty with this kind of narration is that the narrator's representation of events is necessarily subjective. Readers have to judge for themselves whether the narrator's account is reliable or not. Some romance writers and critics believe that third-person central narration allows readers to identify with the heroine, while others assert that women readers actually identify with the hero. According to best-selling author Laura Kinsale, the hero represents an opportunity for women readers to express aggressive feelings and enjoy adventures that are prohibited in their daily lives. Either way, third-person shifting narration affords romance readers a broader perspective on events than first-person narration.

In her two previous novels, *Disappearing Acts* and *Waiting to Exhale*,

McMillan had perfected the technique of using first-person central narration to intimately engage readers in the story. Throughout *Waiting to Exhale*, Savannah's voice addresses readers as if they are close confidantes and invites them into her circle of friends. Stella's first-person central narration achieves the same effect. In fact, the intimate tone of her monologue suggests that it could be addressed to her recently deceased best friend, Delilah. Readers are privileged to hear Stella's most intimate thoughts and feelings, and for most, Stella's candor is compelling.

McMillan had used two first-person central narrators in *Waiting to Exhale*—the perceptive Savannah and the self-deluded Robin. Savannah and Robin functioned as foils for each other in the novel, highlighting the positive and negative choices women make in defining their lives. First-person central narration also enabled McMillan to realistically portray women's psychological motivations for making different choices. In many ways, Stella is a blend of these two characters. On the one hand, her interior monologue exhibits great perceptiveness about a wide range of people and events. Stella shares Savannah's ability to analyze her own motivations honestly. For example, right after meeting Winston, she chastises herself for "getting all shook up over some young boy" (54), yet she is honest enough to recognize that Winston moves her emotionally as well as physically. It would have been much easier for a character in her position to pretend that all she felt was lust.

At the same time, Stella has also embarked on an adventure that completely transcends anything she has experienced in her forty-two years. Thus, she shares Robin's aura of innocence. Some reviewers have commented that Stella's naivete seems implausible in a woman of her years, but the novel is about recapturing the sense of wonder in life. Stella's story also conforms to conventions of the romance genre, which dictate that the hero and heroine must experience their love as a first-time-ever experience, even if they have been happily married before. Readers like to see true love depicted as a previously unimagined dimension of life.

McMillan does, in fact, exploit Stella's naivete to create moments of irony, just as she does with Robin in *Waiting to Exhale*. For example, in one scene, Stella is looking for an interesting book to pass the time until her evening rendezvous with Winston. Among the titles she has brought to Jamaica is *Waiting to Exhale*. Stella says she cannot understand what all the hype is about. She complains that McMillan does not really have a style and asserts that the book has no literary merit. Although she finds that she can relate to some of the characters, she decides she is not in the mood to read about "a bunch of woe-is-me black women" (60). In this passage, McMillan parodies negative criticism of her own work. Further, when Stella says, "the main reason I didn't read this book was because from what I heard a couple of these women sounded too much like me although I'm not as stupid as a few of them," McMillan's dramatic irony springs the joke on Stella. Readers know, although Stella does not, that she is one of McMillan's fictional creations just as are the women in the book. In addition, this dramatic irony makes Stella's assessment of McMillan's work unreliable and, by extension, undermines the judgments of all the critics who said similar things.

On the next page, Stella is dressing for her date. After taking a shower, she boldly decides not to wear panties but sprays on lots of feminine deodorant, then begins a long rant on feminine hygiene that concludes with the rhetorical question, "I mean, can you really smell too clean?" (62). Several critics have attacked McMillan for including such a "self-hating" passage in the book. Such misunderstanding is what comes of taking ironic statements literally. Stella does indeed think this way. Her sermon on feminine hygiene reveals some of her basic insecurities and also shows how nervous she is before her date with Winston. Stella, however, is McMillan's fictional creation. They share the experience of having traveled to Jamaica and of having fallen in love with much younger men, but their values and beliefs are not necessarily the same.

In this instance, FDS (feminine deodorant spray) is a famous feminist controversy. When this product appeared in the 1970s, feminists attacked it as a symbol of how women are taught to hate their bodies and devalue themselves. Stella's rant is ridiculously exaggerated. Thus, through hyperbolic humor, McMillan pokes fun at Stella's thinking at the same time that she baits hard-line feminists who had argued the opposite position vociferously. Some reviewers have lamented that McMillan departed from her usual irreverent irony in *How Stella Got Her Groove Back*. But for readers who understand how she is manipulating the codes of popular romance, the novel still resonates with her trademark humor. Indeed, one message of the whole novel is the importance of not taking oneself or life too seriously.

Nevertheless, McMillan also uses irony to invite readers to think seriously about various issues. Corinne O. Nelson, who reviewed the novel for the May 15, 1996, issue of *Library Journal*, complained that "nothing here convinces the reader that the island is an exotic vacation spot." Stella does take authentic pleasure in the beach, the sun, the clear water, and the majesty of the Blue Mountains. When she goes on a horseback tour, however, she becomes aware of other vistas. Stella had pictured herself galloping along the beach, but her tour guide leads her on a two-hour trek through the mountains instead. She is disturbed by the living conditions she observes along the way. They pass communities that have no roads, no electricity, no running water, and no septic tanks. Stella does not want to believe that families actually live in the flimsy little shacks she sees.

Stella remains incredulous, but this line of thinking makes her recall old photos of her grandparents sitting on porches in front of shacks much like the ones she sees in Jamaica. Her reaction is to wish she could "get off this damn horse and sit down under a tree and find an ice-cold bottle of Evian or Crystal Geyser with lime" (77). Here the ironic distance between McMillan and her naive narrator highlights Stella's shallow consumerism. "Designer water" has become a symbol of conspicuous consumption. Wishing for such consumer comforts is clearly an inappropriate response to the realities Stella has just witnessed. By including this passage, McMillan gently pokes fun at Stella and at naive tourists who share her mentality. Further, by depriving Stella and readers of a picturesque gallop along the beach, McMillan has resisted a long tradition of exoticism in popular romance while sketching connections between economic exploitation at home and abroad.

CHARACTER DEVELOPMENT

Waiting to Exhale featured four main characters, but *How Stella Got Her Groove Back* has only one fully developed character—Stella. Her erotic response to Winston conveys details about his appearance to readers. He is tall and lean with long arms, which Stella likes to imagine wrapped around her. She notices his clean, citrusy cologne and later seeks to purchase some so that she can reexperience his presence at will. The dialogue passages give readers an idea of his speech, but the narrative does not allow access to his thoughts. Nor do his actions drive the plot. He is sure from the beginning that he wants to be with Stella. If he has doubts, readers do not get to hear them. Consequently, as with the male characters in *Waiting to Exhale*, Winston is not fully developed because it is Stella's story.

As she did with Savannah, McMillan lets Stella tell readers what she looks like as she selects clothes for different occasions. Descriptions of clothes are important in the romance genre. Women readers enjoy details of color, line, and texture. Women are also accustomed to choosing and reading clothes as social masks. They understand the profound symbolism a heroine's clothes can convey. For example, when she goes to the pajama disco with Winston, Stella wears a white nightgown. The gown expresses the innocence and purity she experiences in this new romance. At the same time, when she stands in the light it is transparent, and she decides to leave her panties in her hotel room. In this costume, she is ready to risk loving with both body and soul.

Like the women in *Waiting to Exhale*, Stella's living quarters reflect much about who she is. Her house is even more sumptuous than Bernadine's. Where the décor in Bernadine's house symbolizes her capitulation to her husband's taste, Stella's medley of colors and textures shows that she is an independent woman of substance as well as a very creative person. Bernadine's struggle with her ex-husband had given *Waiting to Exhale* dramatic impetus, but the plot of *How Stella Got Her Groove Back* is basically uneventful. Stella's thoughts and feelings take up more narrative space than her actions. Yet her actions show her growing willingness to take risks and reach for happiness. For example, when she finally decides to send Winston a plane ticket so that he can visit her in the United States, she comes to her travel agent's office armed with a prepaid, preaddressed Federal Express envelope. She mails the ticket before getting in her car to go home.

Critics who have complained that the plot is too predictable or does not provide sufficient conflict have misunderstood two key aspects of the text. The first is that McMillan is revising the popular romance form, which dictates a happy ending. For romance readers, how the characters reach this destination is the important thing. The fact that the hero and heroine will end up together should never really be in question. The other issue is that, for McMillan's purposes, characterizing Stella through her thoughts is more important than characterizing her through her actions.

Throughout the novel, Stella continually resolves to take action and then pushes herself to follow through before she can change her mind. The first-person central narration makes readers privy to all Stella's thoughts. Her insecurities and inhibitions are clearly visible. In this way, McMillan humanizes Stella and dramatizes her decision-making processes. Thus, another reason that the plot is not action-packed is that the process of deciding what action to take is more important for Stella's growth than the actions she takes as a result.

Stella's narrative voice not only gives readers direct access to her thoughts, it also acquaints them with her unique personal style. Like Savannah, her language resonates with urban black vernacular rhythms and rhetorical figures. McMillan had minimized the use of nonstandard grammatical structures even in the dialogue passages of *Waiting to Exhale*. Here, in contrast, some structures that are common in black vernacular speech do find their way into Stella's speech. One example appears during a conversation with her sister, where Stella uses a black English construction of "be": "Vanessa, don't be telling people all my personal business" (34). Reflecting on conversations with her sister, Stella explains that "we always change our voices like we're from or been living deep in the hood all our lives, like we're young and hip and not even close to being educated" (32). Linguists call such patterns of shifting between languages or dialects "code switching."

Speakers who command both a prestige language such as standard English and a low-status code such as black English or Spanish in the United States tend to use the code in private, intimate conversations. Using the low-status code expresses solidarity and endearment within the sociolinguistic in-group. It also expresses the speaker's identification with a specific ethnolinguistic heritage. This is why even well-educated speakers of low-status codes are frequently unwilling to give them up. Like Stella, they use language as a sign that they have not forgotten their roots. Stella's code switching shows that even though she is successful in the white corporate world, she is "down" with her African American cultural heritage. As in *Waiting to Exhale*, Stella's language does not exclude readers from other backgrounds, but it speaks most directly to McMillan's core audience of African Americans by highlighting the perspective of a strong, independent African American woman.

LITERARY STYLE

Stella's first-person central narration follows a form known as "stream of consciousness." This technique is intended to represent the associative patterns of thoughts as they flit through the mind. Many reviewers have criticized McMillan's handling of this technique, particularly because she chose to delete most of the internal punctuation from her sentences. Yet there is a method and an artistic rationale for this seeming "madness." McMillan's experimentation with punctuation consists primarily of deleting commas that would normally separate items in a list: "I hate going to Home Depot because I always end up going down the plant rug toilet

or sink aisles when I have enough plants rugs toilets and sinks already"
(2). Stella may sound like she is babbling on and on, but this impression
results from McMillan's careful craft.

McMillan sets herself an even greater challenge by casting the entire
stream-of-consciousness narration in the present tense. Most novice writers have a hard time mastering tense structure within narration. Shifting
into the present tense to make a particular action or feeling more vivid
is a technique people commonly use in speech: "So yesterday I went to
the grocery store because I'm out of milk and there I am waiting in this
long line when this guy taps me on the shoulder and asks if he can cut
in front of me because he only has three items and I have four. Well I
told him . . ." But when writers shift back and forth between present and
past tense like this within a story, readers easily become confused. Trying
to narrate an entire story in present tense adds other problems. Indicating that an action happened before some other action in the past with
the simple past and the past perfect is a familiar construction: "Everyone
had eaten [past perfect] by the time Jack showed up [simple past]." Describing this sequence of events in the present tense sounds unnatural:
"Everyone has eaten [present perfect] by the time Jack shows [simple
present] up." Although this construction is grammatically correct, inex-
perienced writers tend to mix up the tense harmony and produce sentences like, "Everyone had eaten by the time Jack shows up." Sustaining
present tense narration for 368 pages while Stella reflects on her past,
present, and future shows McMillan's formal control. Overall, the prose
rhythm she establishes invites readers to get caught up in the moment
with Stella. Once the reader is "in the groove," the unusual style is not
confusing at all.

In fact, the first-person, present tense, stream-of-consciousness narration draws readers into Stella's adventure. It forces them to experience
the events with Stella in "real time." Yet the first line of the novel—"I
hadn't planned on going anywhere"—indicates that Stella is actually
describing events that have already happened. This makes the whole
story an artistic creation. McMillan thus frames the novel so that it is
conceivably Stella's choice to shift the narration into the present tense
for dramatic effect, the way everyday people do when describing their
experiences to friends. Thus, one important aspect of how Stella gets her
groove back is the artistic shaping she applies to her story in the process
of telling it.

The rhetorical strategy of empowering oneself through "narrative sequencing" or storytelling has antecedents in both vernacular and literary

traditions within African American culture. In the vernacular tradition, as is the case with McMillan's other works, Stella's story works in the narrative sequencing mode known as "testifyin'." As noted earlier, the purpose of testifyin' is to tell the truth through stories, to artfully represent experience so that others can identify with and affirm it. In *How Stella Got Her Groove Back*, perhaps the most autobiographical of her novels, McMillan is testifying through a fictionalized account of her own experience. Still, McMillan could have written an equally autobiographical story without framing it as the protagonist's testimonial. Thus, the form in which McMillan casts the story metaphorically figures the thematic content, which is the regeneration of artistic desire.

In a conversation with her sister Vanessa soon after her return from Jamaica, Stella rants about youth violence and emphatically expresses the opinion that all children should be exposed to *The Autobiography of Malcolm X* in the third grade. Vanessa replies, "You should've been an evangelist in a church for the fucking profane" (134), summing up, in essence, the function of Stella's narrative. She testifies about experiences that, in the Judeo-Christian belief system, fall under the category of the "profane." Nevertheless, her testimonial on the power of love recognizes it as a transformative spiritual force in the way that Afro-centric cosmology has always regarded it. Stella's testimonial, therefore, follows the blues rather than the gospel mode. Her narration is a verbal performance that functions like the songs Zora wanted to write in *Disappearing Acts*: it makes the audience feel glad to be alive. Further, in this blues performance tradition, the idiosyncrasies of Stella's style, particularly the lack of punctuation, work the way that an improvised solo does. The free-flowing sentences are like the cascades of notes that Charlie Parker, John Coltrane, and Miles Davis would rain down on their audiences when they were testifyin' about "a love supreme" with their horns.

Like all McMillan's fiction, *How Stella Got Her Groove Back* is well rooted in African American oral performance traditions. At the same time, the most obvious literary antecedent for this blues testimonial on the power of love is Zora Neale Hurston's *Their Eyes Were Watching God*. McMillan's narrative frame follows the model of Janie's testimonial to her friend Phoeby in that book. Having been "a delegate to de big 'ssociation of life" (18), Janie is bursting with a lifetime of experience to share. At the end of her story, she and Phoeby conclude, "you got to go there to know there," but the act of telling Phoeby "where she is coming from" gives Janie the ultimate creative power to define her own life. Similarly, while Stella has a love story to tell, the act of telling that story puts her back in her creative groove because storytelling itself is a form of creativity.

THEMATIC ISSUES: REGENERATING THE ARTISTIC SELF

The major theme of the novel is the creative process and the role of the artist in society. This theme occurs throughout McMillan's work. In *Mama*, Freda gradually learns the discipline she needs to succeed as a writer. As a journalist, she seeks to use her writing to expose the truth to a mass audience. In *Waiting to Exhale*, Savannah is not content with a high-paying job. She seeks the challenge of doing creative work. Thus, she accepts a big pay cut in order to break into producing television shows. Franklin and Zora in *Disappearing Acts* are both self-identified artists. Franklin is a talented woodworker who views his custom-built pieces of furniture as works of art. Zora is a singer and songwriter who hopes to touch people and uplift their spirits with her music. Stella emerges as a blend of these two characters' artistic goals.

As a young woman, Stella had earned her M.F.A. and had used this training to design unique pieces of furniture. Like Franklin, she regards these creations as "functional sculpture." In telling her story, she also engages in an oral performance analogous to Zora's singing. Further, her story culminates in a happy ending, and thus it offers a message of hope akin to what Zora wanted to convey through her music. McMillan herself has said that she believes the purpose of literature is to give people hope (Fitchner). Hence, she shares with her characters a highly functional vision of art; consequently, her pragmatic goals for her own work help explain her appeal to the mass audience. Her work serves an immediate purpose in the lives of her many readers, one that a more specifically "literary" writer such as Toni Morrison could not hope to fulfill. McMillan's credentials, the innovative complexity of her technique, and her continuing discourse on the role of the artist in society all indicate that she is capable of producing work that would satisfy the criteria of a literary aesthetic. Her decision to write for the mass audience is thus an artistic choice.

The theme of artistic creation operates on more than one level in *How Stella Got Her Groove Back*. The novel is popularly known as a reverse of the typical May/December romance, yet what really puts Stella back "in the groove" is her reconnection with her own artistic desire. At the most basic level, the theme of artistic creation pervades Stella's thoughts throughout the novel. On the book's opening pages, Stella looks out across her yard, sees the storage shed that used to be her studio, and regretfully remembers when she used to be creative. She explains in this passage that she could not figure out "how to mix commerce with art" and therefore gave up her artwork (3–4). Nevertheless, Stella's house is a collage of colors and textures, a fact that makes her proud that she had decorated her home to suit her unique taste.

Stella later explains that she works as a financial analyst because it is difficult to win serious recognition as an artist, but her ability to manipulate numbers yields more tangible rewards. Stella is bored with her job and wishes for a new direction but does not know how to make room in her life for her art: "I've always been good at making things that serve a purpose, that perform, that function but art is so iffy" (16) she demurs. Yet this statement clearly expresses her functionalist vision of art. Stella's alienation from the creative process does not come from any fear that art is too esoteric and removed from the more meaningful strata of life. Further, these remarks indicate that even before she meets Winston, she actively seeks to reconnect with her own creative energy. Like Savannah in *Waiting to Exhale*, Stella has plenty to say about her loneliness, her disappointment with her ex-husband, and her doubts about the institution of marriage. Still, she is not looking for love to cure her general disaffection. Rather, she sees the lack of love in her life as symptomatic of a deeper lack of meaning and direction.

The natural beauty of Jamaica helps Stella begin this reconnection with her own creative energy. During her horseback trek through the mountains, she experiences a spiritual epiphany. Her thoughts about how to communicate this beauty to others are a glimpse into her understanding of the artistic process. She says she is glad she did not bring a camcorder or camera to capture the view because too much of the experience would be lost. Instead, she is thankful that she can preserve the moment in her memory and asks only that she be able to describe enough of the beauty to entice other people to want to experience it themselves. Since Stella's entire narrative functions as a testimonial, this comment expresses her general motivation for telling the story of how she got her groove back. Maybe she will inspire other people to seek a similar experience for themselves.

When Stella returns from Jamaica, her friends and family clearly see that she is different. Her sister Angela fears that she has lost her head over Winston and is behaving irrationally. When Stella tells her that she does not want to look for another job as a securities analyst, Angela sarcastically remarks on Stella's apparent decision to pursue something more "creative" and "fulfilling." Her comments are intended facetiously, but Stella responds that this is exactly how she feels. She also rejects the notion that sleeping with Winston is wholly responsible for her new attitude. This exchange highlights the primary importance of artistic creation as a means of spiritual regeneration in the novel. Love is simply an added attraction in Stella's quest to reorient her life.

As Stella risks a deeper connection with Winston, her connection with her artistic desire also deepens. Soon after her second visit to Jamaica, she flies to San Diego to visit her friend Maisha, who owns an art gallery. Stella brings her a hand-knitted sweater made of copper thread. Maisha raves over this piece of "wearable art" and insists on displaying it in the gallery, where it attracts a lot of interest from the patrons. At the gallery, Stella arranges to purchase a piece that looks like a vintage photograph of a black family. She also networks with a male artist who lives near her in the Bay Area. When Stella tells Maisha she has been fired from her job, Maisha thinks it is a good thing because now Stella can finally be the artist she was meant to be (292). Overall, the trip to the gallery reconnects Stella both emotionally and professionally with the art world. When Winston finally arrives, he adds his support to the direction Stella has already chosen.

Winston's first impression of Stella's home reconfirms her identity as an artist. He appreciates her furniture as sculpture. After touring the house, he takes an immediate interest in cleaning up her studio, starting with her drafting table because, as he says, "you'll be using this" (343). Stella's ex-husband had encouraged her to earn her graduate degree in business administration. In doing so, he had helped alienate her from her art. In contrast, Winston recognizes that Stella is an artist the minute he steps inside her home. His response to her makes her feel like crying because she cannot remember when someone last made her feel that good about herself (343). In several sensuous passages, Stella describes how good making love with Winston makes her feel, but his validation of her artistic identity touches her more deeply than anything else. Indeed, no sooner has he pledged to clean out the studio for her than he offers to drive her directly to her favorite art supply store.

During Winston's visit, he continually encourages Stella to work on her art. After he has cleaned out her studio, Stella says she will wait until he leaves so she can focus on her work, but Winston tells her to stop focusing on him. While Franklin pays for Zora to get her piano out of storage in *Disappearing Acts*, once she gets wrapped up in practicing and writing new songs, he begins to resent that she is no longer fully focused on him. Winston is not threatened by Stella's wealth, her age, or her creative power. He is an ideal lover, and, yet, when the title phrase occurs in the novel, it is in reference to reconnecting with artistic inspiration, not to "sexual healing." On page 361 Stella says, "... it's hard getting your groove back once you've lost it," but Winston refuses to accept her excuses for not pursuing her art.

ALTERNATIVE INTERPRETATION: ARCHETYPAL CRITICISM

Authors often represent universal human experiences like romantic love in terms of well-known figures such as Romeo and Juliet, the star-crossed lovers. Archetypal criticism analyzes such universal symbols and assesses how skillfully an author invites readers to relate their own experiences to those of a fictional hero and/or heroine. Authors may also use archetypal symbols to teach a moral lesson. For example, Aesop's famous fable about the tortoise and the hare presents two personality types that everyone is familiar with in order to demonstrate that the slow, steady approach is more effective in the long run. This type of story is known as an allegory. On the surface, *How Stella Got Her Groove Back* is a love story with universal appeal. Yet a deeper reading of the text uncovers the theme of artistic creation working at many levels. In fact, McMillan manipulates elements of the romance genre in order to develop an allegorical reflection on the artistic process in her novel.

Best-selling romance authors Linda Barlow and Jayne Ann Krentz argue that popular romance satisfies readers by continually re-enacting certain archetypal myths, that is, stories which symbolically speak to universal human experiences. They assert that the most popular of these myths is marriage with the devil ("Beneath the Surface"). Novels based on models such as the classical Greek myth of Persephone, who was kidnapped by the lord of the underworld, consistently outsell all other plot variations. On the one hand, Barlow and Krentz believe that the marriage-with-the-devil story expresses women's feelings about teaching their partners to temper the patriarchal values of aggression and confrontation with compassion and tenderness. Thus, this age-old archetype holds universal appeal. On the other hand, Barlow and Krentz also assert that romance writers and readers are much better educated than has been commonly assumed. Barlow, for example, holds a master's in English literature and had begun a doctoral dissertation on "Feminist Voices in Eighteenth and Nineteenth Century English Romances" before she decided to pursue a full-time career as a novelist. Thus, romance writers often deliberately incorporate references to mythology into their novels and can reasonably expect that many readers will recognize a heroine named "Prosperina" as a copy of Persephone (Barlow and Krentz 22). And Krentz is especially skilled at structuring her novels as allegorical commentary on women's fiction and the institution of patriarchal marriage, even as she weaves an engaging and entertaining story.

Literary critics usually assume that romance writers are primarily motivated by the desire to make money. Several reviewers have suggested that *How Stella Got Her Groove Back* was something "quick and dirty" McMillan produced to satisfy her publisher and fans. Yet Krentz has proved that popular romance can be a vehicle for demonstrating technical virtuosity as a writer, for reflecting on the function of literature in women's lives, and for commenting on social realities. Thus, an archetypal reading of the artistic creation theme in *How Stella Got Her Groove Back* is justified.

Black female readers probably enjoy stories based on the marriage-with-the-devil archetype as much as anyone else. Yet, following in Zora Neale Hurston's footsteps, the most powerful archetype in black women writers' representation of love is an older woman's romance with a younger man who teaches her to laugh and enjoy life. Hurston's Teacake does this for Janie in *Their Eyes Were Watching God*; Gloria Naylor's George teaches Cocoa to play in *Mama Day*, even though he is older than she is; Tina McElroy Ansa's Herman reconnects Lena with all varieties of sensual pleasure in *The Hand I Fan With*; and McMillan's Winston rekindles Stella's artistic as well as erotic desire. Jungian analysis can help explain why the older woman/younger man theme is so much more compelling than the marriage-with-the-devil archetype for black women writers.

Carl Gustav Jung (1875–1961), a Swiss psychiatrist who extended Sigmund Freud's approach to psychoanalysis, broke with Freud's narrow interpretation of the libido (the sexual drive) as the primary motivation for human behavior in 1912, when he published *Psychology of the Unconscious*. Jung believed that sexual drives were only one aspect of human beings' overall quest to express their creative energy. He regarded mythology as a symbolic repository of these creative urges and developed a theory explaining how the archetypes found in myths are invested with emotions, thoughts, and memories universally shared by all human beings. He called this theory the "collective unconscious." Jungian analysts interpret myths, fantasies, dreams, fairy tales, and literature to help their clients achieve mental and spiritual well-being. Literary critics have found Jung's analysis of archetypal symbols useful for developing a deeper understanding of literary texts.

A Jungian analysis of black women writers' representations of transformative love must ask what the figures of the world-weary older woman and the carefree younger man represent in the collective experience of black women. Jungian analyst Linda Schierse Leonard proposes that all women have been wounded to some degree by the collective authority of patriarchal society as well as by the individual dynamics of the father-daughter relationship. In her book *The Wounded Woman*, she identifies several different personality adaptations to these wounds, drawing on examples from mythology, literature, and film as well as from her clinical practice. The world-weary older women who appear in black women's best-known novels about romantic love correspond to a type Leonard identifies as "the armored amazon." Leonard likens this type to the amazons of classical mythology, who regarded men as contemptible weaklings and who trained themselves to be fierce warriors, even amputating their right breasts so that they could shoot arrows more accurately. According to Leonard, the armored amazon strives to follow a masculine model of strength and power as a reaction against the collective or individual irresponsibility of the men in her life. Leonard points out that while many women have been wounded by the weaknesses of their individual fathers, patriarchal society as a whole devalues the feminine principle. Therefore, even women who had good relationships with their fathers may react with "armored amazon" rage against the limitations of the acceptable feminine role in society. Nevertheless, this reaction alienates women from their feminine qualities, thereby cutting them off from a source of internal strength.

Each of the women in the above-mentioned quartet of novels has a problematic relationship with her father. Janie's father was a white man who raped her mother. His act of violence also deprived her of her mother, for, in her shame and grief, Janie's mother abandons her child to be raised by her own mother. Cocoa is raised by her two great-aunts because her parents are deceased. Growing up, she has no relationship with a father figure. Lena's father is a prosperous businessman, but he forces her mother to handle his affairs while he consorts with his drinking buddies and other women. Lena's father dotes on her, but his treatment of her mother wounds her. As for Stella, she says that her father disappeared over twenty years ago, and she and her sisters are not interested in finding him.

On top of the wounds inflicted in their individual father-daughter relationships, black women have also been deeply wounded by a collective white-male power structure, which has historically regarded them as unfeminine beasts of burden. Indeed, Janie's grandmother offers this analysis of black women's place in the world:

> Maybe it's some place way off in de ocean where de black man is in power but we don't know nothin' but what we see. So de white man throw down de load and tell de nigger man tuh pick it up. He pick it up because he have to, but he don't tote it. He hand it to his womenfolks. De nigger woman is de mule uh de world so fur as Ah can see. (Hurston 29)

Consequently, even when a black woman has grown up with strong, responsible black men in her life, socioeconomic pressures may turn her into an armored amazon.

Leonard finds that the psychic antidote for the armored amazon is a young male figure who frequently appears in fairy tales—the "dummling." The armored amazon develops many positive traits such as confidence, assertiveness, and accomplishment. Eventually, however, her view of life as an ongoing battle exhausts her, and she loses the sense of meaning she had once found in proving her worth in masculine terms. Yet the amazon has cut herself off from the playful, spontaneous, and imaginative aspects of masculinity, associating them with weakness and irresponsibility. The dummling character in traditional fairy tales is a youth who is continually ridiculed for his weakness and incompetence. Yet his spontaneity often enables him to "stumble" onto the right path, and his ability to acknowledge the limits of his knowledge and strength usually wins him powerful allies who are willing to share their wisdom with him. In the end, the dummling's kindness and good humor allow him to overcome the most impossible trials and win the richest treasures.

Leonard uses her analysis of fairy tales to show the universality of the dummling figure. Then she gives clinical examples from her practice to show how often such characters turn up in the dreams and fantasies of armored amazons. Since romance novels are geared toward articulating women's collective fantasies, it makes sense that the dummling lover is the most compelling ideal for African American armored amazons. Indeed, Janie says that Teacake looks "like women's dreams of love." Teacake, George, Herman, and Winston all manifest dummling traits, only in an African American context, it might be more accurate to describe them as "trifling," since this term carries specific connotations in vernacular black English.

The trifling man is a staple in blues women's laments. Usually a rootless drifter, his belief system rejects family values. He refuses to keep a steady job and has no qualms about living off his woman. Nor does he hesitate to spend her hard-earned money on other women. The trifling man does not believe that education and hard work are the keys to success. Rather, he feels that people who pursue this path are dupes of a racist game, the rules of which are specifically designed to keep them from ever winning. He himself may be a slick trickster who earns his way by gambling or running various hustles on people. The trifling man lives for the moment. Often he has musical talents. Naturally, he is a good dancer, and no one ever has complaints about his skills as a lover. Unfortunately, he can also turn to domestic violence. Leonard might view this kind of acting out as an expression of anger at the collective patriarchal authority, a quality which is the darker aspect of the "dummling," who has been devalued by the patriarchy. Yet, she believes that connecting with this anger is part of what the armored amazon needs in order to reawaken her own creative energy. This need may explain "why a woman loves a heel," as blues diva Dinah Washington, who was legendary for her troubles with "trifling men," put it in a 1946 song.

At first glance, Teacake and Winston definitely look like trifling fellows to Janie's and Stella's friends and associates. Lena's friends and acquaintances also attribute her changed behavior to the influence of some trifling man, but Herman is a ghost whom no one but Lena can see. Metaphorically, this circumstance expresses the fact that only the woman in love can see the positive qualities in a man who everyone else believes is totally unsuitable for her. *Mama Day* offers a seeming contrast in that George is an engineer with his own business. He appears to epitomize responsibility, but a congenital heart defect lends him a dummling kind of weakness. This physical weakness has forced him to develop some of the more playful and spontaneous qualities of the dummling. For example, his courtship of Cocoa consists of walking tours through the varied neighborhoods of New York City. During these explorations, he teaches Cocoa to see people differently and to enjoy the kind of simple pleasures the dummling temperament knows how to appreciate. The dummling or trifling man runs true to type in all four novels, but the fact that Teacake is the most likely model for Winston warrants a closer comparison of what these two characters teach their respective armored amazon partners about the creative process.

Janie first meets Teacake one afternoon when most of the town has gone to a baseball game. Janie has stayed behind to mind the store, and Teacake wanders in, having mistaken the location of the game. Like the archetypal dummling, however, he has stumbled on something even better—he is taken with Janie right away. After buying a pack of cigarettes from her, he jokes around and eventually invites her to play checkers. Janie had never learned how to play, but when Teacake offers to teach her, she is thrilled that "somebody wanted her to play. Somebody thought it natural for her to play" (146). In subsequent weeks, Teacake teaches Janie all about playing. He takes her fishing after midnight, invites her to a church picnic, drives her to baseball games, escorts her to movies and dances, plants flowers in her yard, and shows her how to drive. Most of the town thinks Teacake is courting Janie for her money, but when he asks her to marry him, she is determined to take a chance on love.

Nevertheless, when she leaves town to join him in Jacksonville, she takes along a secret stash of $200 "just in case." One morning, she sends her new husband out to buy fish for breakfast, but he does not return for hours and hours. Janie's money is also missing. She spends a long, anxious day, but when Teacake returns, he entertains her with a story of how he found the money and decided to see what it felt like to be a millionaire for one day. He threw a big party with chicken, macaroni and cheese, free drinks, and a guitar player. In the end, Janie tells him she is angry, not because he spent her money, but because he left her out of a good time. Teacake confesses that he was afraid she would not care for the habits of his laborer friends, but Janie says she wants to share in all of his adventures. This scene is a perfect example of how the trifling man frees the armored amazon from the rigid constraints under which she had been living. Janie comes to a deeper level of trust in the spontaneous, playful qualities which allow Teacake to provide her with such rich experiences. It takes Janie three husbands and over twenty years to complete her quest for psychic fulfillment. Although Teacake occasionally beats her and eventually succumbs to rabies-induced madness, Janie's experiences with him enable her to break through her amazon armor and creatively re-define her life by telling her own story to her best friend.

Winston Shakespeare is not as colorful as Teacake. He comes from a middle-class Jamaican family, and he has completed college. The fact that he does not have a well-defined career plan has more to do with his youth than with a resistance to the traditional work ethic. He is a good dancer, but, unlike Teacake, he is too shy to be the life of anyone's party. Janie follows where Teacake leads, but Stella is much more self-actualized than Janie. Further, she is a first-person central narrator, while Hurston uses a third-person omniscient narrator to portray the events that Janie is presumably recounting to her friend. As a result, the story is more about how Stella comes to risk letting Winston into her life than it is about Winston actively teaching her anything. Nevertheless, his marriage proposal at the end of the novel reprises an important symbol from *Their Eyes Were Watching God.*

On the night when Teacake and Janie become lovers, she finds him "sleeping" in the hammock on her front porch when she comes home from the store. When she approaches to shake him awake, he pulls her in with him. Likewise, just before Winston asks Stella to marry him, he calls her outside and invites her to join him in a hammock. First, she argues that there is not enough room. This excuse mirrors her concerns about making room for him in her life. Then, she protests that she will fall out. Winston says that he has been in the hammock for over an hour and has not fallen out, although he concedes that it does feel like one might. Stella responds that she does not like that feeling (363), but Winston intuitively knows she is referring to a fear of being out of control, not a fear of falling. After he reassures her that he will not let her fall, Stella finally joins him in the hammock, but the fact that she does feel comfortable with Winston scares her even more. She complains that it is too cold outside, so Winston fetches a down comforter, gets back in the hammock, and then initiates the discussion of their future together. In this way, McMillan elaborates for six pages on Hurston's original paragraph, but both hammock scenes symbolize the armored amazon's fear of losing control. In both cases, the trifling man shows the amazon the necessity of giving up control in order to realize a deeper level of comfort. Thus, Teacake and Winston serve the same archetypal function.

Just as the marriage-with-the-devil archetype enables the skilled romance writer to make allegorical commentary on patriarchal marriage, the archetypal romance between the world-weary black woman and the trifling black man also functions as an allegorical reflection on black women's creative processes. Psychic union with the trifling man allows the African American armored amazon to reconnect with the inner qualities that will restore her creative power. Once she has achieved this state of psychic integration, her first imperative is to define or create herself as an empowered human being by telling her own story. Then, she is free to create her art out of her own unique perspective on the world. Lay readers, literary critics, and black women writers alike cherish *Their Eyes Were Watching God* because it is one of the first blueprints describing how African American women can make art out of the substance of their lives. In *How Stella Got Her Groove Back* and throughout her opus, McMillan extends Hurston's celebration of black women inventing their own lives and thereby earns the profound appreciation of a community of readers that transcends race, class, and gender.

Bibliography

WORKS BY TERRY McMILLAN

Breaking Ice: An Anthology of Contemporary African-American Fiction [editor]. New York: Viking Press, 1990.

Disappearing Acts. New York: Viking Press, 1989.

How Stella Got Her Groove Back. New York: Viking Penguin, 1996.

"The Love We've Lost." *Essence*, May 1993, 75+.

Mama. Boston: Houghton Mifflin Company, 1987.

"On My Own Terms." *Essence*, May 1995, 52+.

"Publicizing Your Commercially Published Novel." *Poets & Writers* (January/February 1988).

Waiting to Exhale. New York: Viking Press, 1992.

WORKS ABOUT TERRY McMILLAN

Biographical References

Afronet Books Department. "About Terry McMillan." Web site, accessed August 25, 1998, at: *http://www.afronet.com/BOOKSbooks-mcmillan.html*.

Arts Wire. "The Fourth National Black Writers Conference." Web site, accessed August 25, 1998, at: *http://www.tmn.com/Artswire/black/mcmillan.htm*.

"Book of the Year (1997): Biography: McMillan, Terry." Britannica Online Web site, accessed June 1, 1998 at: *http://www.eb.com:180/cgi-bin/g?DocF-boy/97/ K00445.html.*

Green, Anthony. "McMillan, Terry." Britannica Online Web site, accessed June 1, 1998, at: *http://www.eb.com:180/cgi-bin/g?DocF-micro/726/78.html.*

Hershenson, Karen. "Buoyed by Love, Fame, and Knowledge, Terry McMillan Finally Can Exhale." Knight-Ridder/Tribune News Service, December 20, 1995, 1220k8293.

Konkol, Alison, and Mina Ossei. "Voices from the Gaps: Women Writers of Color: Terry McMillan." University of Minnesota, Department of English Web site, accessed June 1, 1998, at: *http://english.cla.umn.edu/lkd/vfg/Authors/ Terry McMillan.*

Leland, John. "How Terry Got Her Groove." *Newsweek*, April 29, 1996, 76+.

Macon, Wanda. "McMillan, Terry." *The Oxford Companion to African American Literature*, ed. William L. Andrews et al. New York: Oxford UP, 1997.

Malinowski, Sharon, ed. *Black Writers*. Detroit: Gale Research, Inc., 1994.

"Terry McMillan." *Black Writers*, ed. Sharon Malinowski. Detroit: Gale Research, Inc., 1994.

"Terry McMillan." *Modern Black Writers Supplement* 2 (1995).

"Terry McMillan." *People Weekly*, December 28, 1992.

"Terry McMillan." *Who's Who Among African Americans*. New York: Gale Research, Inc., 1997.

Thompson, Kathleen. "McMillan, Terry." In *Black Women in America: An Historical Encyclopedia*, ed. Darlene Clark Hine. Brooklyn, NY: Carlson Publishing, Inc., 1993.

Interviews

"Breathing Easy." *People Weekly*, February 5, 1996.

Chambers, Veronica. "Terry McMillan Goes to Hollywood." *Quarterly Black Review of Books* [online], accessed December 20, 1996, at: *http://www. bookwire.com/qbr/features/95-nov/mcmillan.html.*

"A Conversation with Terry McMillan." *Conduit* [online], accessed July 2, 1998, at: *http://www.theconduit.com/.*

Edwards, Audrey. "Terry McMillan Waiting to Inhale." *Essence*, October 1992, 77+.

Fichtner, Margaria. "Best Seller 'Stella' Has Terry McMillan in a Successful Groove." Knight-Ridder/Tribune News Service, May 29, 1996, 529k8325.

Giles, Molly. "An Interview with Terry McMillan." *Poets & Writers* 20, no. 6 (November/December 1992): 32–43.

Guthman, Edward. "Terry McMillan in the Groove" *San Francisco Chronicle*, February 8, 1998, 38.

Hubbard, Kim, and Penelope Rowlands. "On Top of Her Game." *People Weekly*, April 29, 1996, 111+.

Probst, Ken. "Terry McMillan." *McCall's*, November 1996, 52+.

Randolph, Laura B. "Black America's Hottest Novelist Terry McMillan Exhales and Inhales in a Revealing Interview." *Ebony*, May 1993, 23+.

Smith, Wendy. "Terry McMillan." *Publishers Weekly*, May 11, 1992, 50–51.

Spratling, Cassandra. "How Terry McMillan Got Her Groove Back." Knight-Ridder/Tribune News Service, May 22, 1996, 522k5475.

" 'Stella' in South Africa: Still Looking for Her Groove: Best-Selling Author Terry McMillan Reveals New Details of Art-Imitating-Life Love Affair." *Ebony*, December 1996, 116.

Wilkerson, Isabel. "On Top of the Word." *Essence*, June 1996, 50+.

BOOK REVIEWS

Mama

Awkward, Michael. "Review of *Mama*." *Callaloo* 11, no. 3 (Summer 1998): 649–50.

Blundell, Janet Boyarin. *Library Journal*, January 1987, 108.

Blythe, Will. "Hustling for Dignity." *New York Times Book Review*, February 22, 1987, 11.

Giddings, Paula. *Essence*, March 1987, 28.

New Yorker, March 16, 1987, 104.

Publishers Weekly, November 28, 1986, 65.

Disappearing Acts

O'Meally, Robert G. "The Caged Birds Sings." *Newsday*, April 13, 1986.

Plevak, Linda L. *School Library Journal*, 44 (March 1998): 211.

Sayers, Valerie. "Someone to Walk Over Me." *New York Times*, August 6, 1989, 8.

Zvirin, Stephanie. *Booklist* 94 (March 1, 1998): 1134.

Waiting to Exhale

Canty, Donnella. *English Journal*, April 1996, 86.

Chadwell, Faye A. *Library Journal*, May 1, 1992, 118.

Isaacs, Susan. *New York Times Book Review*, May 31, 1992, 12.

Jackson, Edward M. "Images of Black Males in Terry McMillan's *Waiting to Exhale.*" *MAWA Review* 1 (June 8, 1993): 20–26.

Sellers, Frances Stead. *Times Literary Supplement*, June 1992, 20.

Sokoll, Judy. *School Library Journal* 38: 142.

How Stella Got Her Groove Back

Allen-Taylor, J. Douglas. "A Most Happy Stella." Web site, accessed August 25, 1998, at: *http://www.metroactive.com/papers/metro/07.03.96/books2–9627.html.*

Ferguson, Sarah. *New York Times Book Review*, June 2, 1996, 21.

Harrison, Katherine. Web site, accessed June 1, 1998, at: *http://www.bookpage.com.*

Kennedy, Dana. *Entertainment Weekly*, May 3, 1996, 70+.

Lewis, Lillian. *Booklist* 92 (April 15, 1996): 1394+.

Nelson, Corinne O. *Library Journal*, May 15, 1996: 84.

Publishers Weekly, April 1, 1996: 52.

Sellers, Frances Stead. *Times Literary Supplement*, November 6, 1992, 20.

Skow, John. "Some Groove." *Time*, May 6, 1996, 77+.

Turner, Paige. "Following Your Bliss, McMillan Style." Web site, accessed August 25, 1998, at: *http://www.frasernet.com/felbli.htm.*

Valentine, Victoria. "Terry McMillan, Back in the Groove." *Emerge*, June 1996, 69–70.

Wartik, Nancy. *Mademoiselle*, July 1996, 77.

FILM REVIEWS

Waiting to Exhale

Ansen, David. *Newsweek*, January 8, 1996, 68.

Assegai, Kuba O. "One Brother's Perspective on the Film *Waiting to Exhale.*" Web site, accessed August 25, 1998, at: *http://www.webcom.com/nattyreb/iostorm/iostorm4.html.*

Chapman, Audrey B. "Exhaling and Inhaling: A Symposium." *Ebony*, April 1996, 116+.

Cheshire, Godfrey. "Waiting to Exhale." *Variety*, December 18, 1995, 66.

Corliss, Richard. *Time*, January 8, 1996, 72.

Dahl, Remington. *Remington Review* [online], accessed August 25, 1998, at: *http://www.movie-reviews.com/exhale.htm.*

Ebert, Roger. *Chicago Sun-Times* [online], December 22, 1995, accessed August 25, 1998, at: *http://www.suntimes.com/ebert/ebert_reviews/1995/12/1212565.html.*

Johnson, Robert E. "Whitney Houston, Angela Bassett, Lela Rochon, Loretta De-
vine Star in 'Waiting to Exhale.' " *Jet*, December 25, 1995, 22+.

Kennedy, Dana. *Entertainment Weekly*, December 22, 1995, 60+.

Norment, Lynn. "Whitney Houston, Angela Bassett Share Joys and Pains in
'Waiting to Exhale.' " *Ebony*, December 1995, 24+.

Rozen, Leah. *People Weekly*, January 8, 1996, 22.

Samuels, Allison, and Jerry Adler. "One for the Sistahs." *Newsweek*, January 8,
1996, 66+.

Tucker, Ken. *Entertainment Weekly*, January 12, 1996, 40.

Vincent, Mal. "Bassett Is Breath of Life in 'Waiting to Exhale.' " *Virginian-Pilot*,
December 27, 1995, E1.

How Stella Got Her Groove Back

Adams, Thelma. " 'Groove'-Y Kind of Luv." *New York Post* [online], accessed
January 30, 1999, at: *http://www.nypostonline.com/reviews/movies/4658.htm*.

Arnold, William. " 'Stella' Is a Missed Opportunity." *Seattle Post-Intelligencer* [on-
line], accessed January 30, 1999, at: *http://entertainmentnewsdaily.com/
IMDS%7CENDMOVIE . . . /4542–0775-pat ___nytimes%7C%7*.

Byerley, Jim. Review of *How Stella Got Her Groove Back*. *Max Reviewer* [online],
accessed January 30, 1999, at: *http://www.cinemax.com/reviews/stella.shtml*.

Corliss, Richard. "Getting in the Groove." *Time* [online], August 17, 1998, accessed January 30, 1999, at: *http://cgi.pathfinder.com/time/magazine/1998/dom/
980817/the___arts.cinema.gettig___11.html*.

Ebert, Roger. Review of *How Stella Got Her Groove Back*. *Chicago Sun-Times* [on-
line], accessed January 30, 1999, at: *http://www.suntimes.com/ebert___reviews/
1998/08/081402.html*.

Holden, Stephen. " 'How Stella Got Her Groove Back': He Likes Video Games?
Nobody's Perfect." *New York Times* [online], August 14, 1998, accessed
January 30, 1999, at: *http://www.nytimes.com/library/film/08148stella-
filmreview.html*.

Hornaday, Ann. "A Good 'Groove.' " *SunSpot* [online], August 8, 1998, accessed
January 30, 1999, at: *http://citysearch.sunspot.net/E/M/BLAMD/0000/00/57*.

Hury, Hadley. Review of *How Stella Got Her Groove Back*. *Memphis Flyer* [online],
August 24, 1998, accessed January 30, 1999, at: *http://weeklywire.com/film-
vault/memphis/h/howstellagothergr1.html*.

Long, Tom. " 'Stella' Goes for the Heart." *Detroit News* [online], August 14, 1998,
accessed January 30, 1999, at: *http://detnews.com/SCREENS/9808/
14/Stella/stella.htm*.

Matthews, Jack. "What's Locale Got to Do with Them?/'Stella,' 'Paradise' Are
Well-Traveled." *Newsday* [online], accessed January 30, 1999, at: *http://
www.newsday.com/movies/rnmxz0f6.htm*.

Murray, Steve. "Bassett Redeems Trip to Vapid 'Groove' Land." *AccessAtlanta* [online], accessed January 30, 1999, at: *http://www.accessatlanta.com/entertainment/movies/reviews/stella_groove.html*.

Siskel, Gene. " 'Stella' Has Problems in Paradise." *Chicago Tribune* [online], August 14, 1998, accessed January 30, 1999, at: *http://chicagotribune.com/leisure/movies/article/0,1051,ART-13162,00.html*.

Stein, Ruthe. " 'Stella' Stuck in a Groove: McMillan Adaptation Overemphasizes Age." *San Francisco Chronicle*, [online], August 14, 1998, accessed January 30, 1999, at: *http://www.sfgate.com/cgi-bin/article.cgi?file=/chronicle/archive/1998/08/14/DD31545.DTL*.

Sterritt, David. "Two Dramas Take on Social, Cultural Differences." *Christian Science Monitor* [online], August 14, 1998, accessed January 30, 1999, at: *http://www.csmonitor.com/durable/1998/08/14/p53sl.htm*.

Strauss, Bob. " 'Stella' Ripples with Romance."*Los Angeles Daily News* [online], accessed January 30, 1999, at: *http://entertainmentnewsdaily.com/IMDS%7CENDMOVIE . . . /4547–0780-pat_nytimes%7C%7*.

Turan, Kenneth. "Well, Isn't It Rather Obvious?" *Los Angeles Times* [online], August 14, 1998, accessed January 30, 1999, at: *http://www.calendarlive.com/HOME/CALENDARLIVE/HOLD/stella_review.htm*.

Wagner, Venise. " 'Stella' Bridges Age Gap." *San Francisco Examiner* [online], August 14, 1998, accessed January 30, 1999, at: *http://www.sfgate.com/cgi-bin/article.cgi?file=/examiner/archive/1998/08/14/WEEKEND8364.dtl*.

Wloszczyna, Susan. "Sleek, Spicy 'Stella': Love Is a Beach." *USA Today* [online], accessed January 30, 1999, at: *http://www.usatoday.com/life/enter/movies/lfilm226.htm*.

OTHER SECONDARY SOURCES

Alcott, Louisa May. *Little Women*. New York: Penguin Books, 1989.

Alvarez, Julia. *How the Garcia Girls Lost Their Accents*. New York: Plume, 1992.

Anderson, Benedict. *Imagined Communities*. New York: Verso, 1991.

Ansa, Tina McElroy. *The Hand I Fan With*. New York: Doubleday, 1996.

Baldwin, James. *If Beale Street Could Talk*. New York: Dell, 1974.

Barlow, Linda, and Jayne Ann Krentz. "Beneath the Surface: The Hidden Codes of Romance." In *Dangerous Men and Adventurous Women*, ed. Jayne Ann Krentz. Philadelphia: Pennsylvania UP, 1992.

Book Wire. "Terry McMillan Performance on *Publishers Weekly* Hardcover Fiction Bestseller List." Web site, accessed August 25, 1998, at: *http://www.bookwire.com/Bookinfo.Author$247*.

Chesnutt, Charles W. *The Conjure Woman*. Ann Arbor: Michigan UP, 1969.

Chodorow, Nancy. "Being and Doing: A Cross-Cultural Examination of the Socialization of Males and Females." In *Woman in Sexist Society: Studies in*

Power and Powerlessness, ed. Vivian Gornick and Barbara K. Moran. New York: New American Library, 1971.

Dandridge, Rita B. "Debunking the Motherhood Myth in Terry McMillan's *Mama.*" *CLA Journal*, June 1998, 405–16.

Daniel, Max. "McMillan's Millions." *New York Times Book Review*, August 9, 1992, 20.

Davis, Thulani. "Don't Worry, Be Buppie: Black Novelists Head for the Mainstream." *Village Voice Literary Supplement*, May 1990, 26–29.

Dinnerstein, Dorothy. *The Mermaid and the Minotaur*. New York: Harper & Row Publishers, 1976.

Du Bois, W. E. B. *The Seeds of Black Folk*. Edited by David Blight and Robert Gooding-Williams. Boston: Bedford Books, 1997.

Esdaile, Leslie. *Sundance*. New York: Kensington, 1996.

Friday, Nancy. *My Mother/My Self*. New York, Dell, 1977.

———. *My Secret Garden*. New York: Pocket Books, 1973.

Garner, Dwight. "Sistahood Is Lucrative."*Salon* [online], accessed March 22, 1998, at: *http://www.salon1999.com/weekly/blacklit960923.html.*

Gregory, Deborah. "The Waiting Game: An Inside Look at How Terry McMillan's Best-Seller Became the 'Sister Film' of the Decade." *Essence*, December 1995, 74+.

Gutman, Herbert G. *The Black Family in Slavery and Freedom: 1750–1925*. New York: Vintage Books, 1976.

Hite, Shere. *The Hite Report on Female Sexuality*. New York: Macmillan Publishing Company, 1976.

Hubbard, Kim. "Little Sister Act." *People Weekly*, April 1, 1996, 107+.

———. "Terry McMillan's New Book *How Stella Got Her Groove Back* to Become Movie." *Jet*, April 29, 1996, 65.

Hughes, Langston, and Mercer Cook, trans. *Masters of the Dew*, by Jacques Roumain. Chicago: Heinemann, 1978.

Hurston, Zora Neale. *Their Eyes Were Watching God*. Urbana: Illinois UP, 1978.

"Interracial Marriages Rising, Says Census Bureau." *Jet*, April 14, 1994, 16.

Jaffe, Rona. *Class Reunion*. New York: Dell, 1979.

Jensen, Margaret Ann. *Love's Sweet Return: The Harlequin Story*. Bowling Green, OH: Bowling Green State UP, 1984.

Jones, Jr., Malcolm. "Successful Sisters: Faux Terry Is Better Than No Terry." *Newsweek*, April 29, 1996, 79.

Kinsale, Laura. "The Androgynous Reader: Point of View in the Romance." In *Dangerous Men and Adventurous Women*, ed. Jayne Ann Krentz. Philadelphia: Pennsylvania UP, 1992.

Kitt, Sandra. *Adam and Eva*. New York: Harlequin Books, 1985.

Leonard, Linda Schierse. *The Wounded Woman*. Boulder, CO: Shambala, 1983.

Levine, Lawrence W. *Black Culture and Black Consciousness*. New York: Oxford UP, 1977.

Major, Clarence. *Juba to Jive: A Dictionary of African-American Slang*. New York: Penguin Books, 1994.

McDowell, Deborah E. Introduction. *Four Girls at Cottage City*, by Emma D. Kelley-Hawkins. New York: Oxford UP, 1989.

McLaughlin, Steven D., et al. *The Changing Lives of American Women*. Chapel Hill: North Carolina UP, 1976.

Mitchell-Powell, Brenda. "The Trouble with Success." *Publishers Weekly*, December 12, 1994, 33+.

Modleski, Tania. *Loving with a Vengeance: Mass Produced Fantasies for Women*. Hamden, CT: Archon Books, 1982.

Nathan, Paul. "Poised for Takeoff." *Publishers Weekly*, March 18, 1996, 25.

Naylor, Gloria. *Mama Day*. New York: Vintage Books, 1989.

O'Brien, Maureen. "Waiting to Publish: Viking Gears Up to 'Crash Produce' Terry McMillan's Newest Novel." *Publishers Weekly*, February 19, 1996, 124.

Petry, Ann. *The Street*. Boston: Beacon Press, 1985.

"Planned Protest Halts Book Signing." *Bookselling This Week* [online] June 30, 1997, accessed August 25, 1998, at: *http://www.bookweb.org/news/bew/787.html*.

Ploski, Harry A., and James Williams, eds. *The Negro Almanac*. Detroit: Gale Research, Inc., 1989.

Polite, Carlene Hatcher. *The Flagellants*. Boston: Beacon Press, 1987.

Pryse, Marjorie. Introduction. *Conjuring: Black Women, Fiction, and Literary Tradition*, ed. Marjorie Pryse and Hortense J. Spillers. Bloomington: Indiana UP, 1985.

Raboteau, Albert J. *Slave Religion*. New York: Oxford UP, 1978.

Radway, Janice. *Reading the Romance: Women, Patriarchy, and Popular Literature*. Chapel Hill: North Carolina UP, 1984.

Randolph, Laura B. "Me as I Wanna Be (Or How to Get Your Groove Back)." *Ebony*, July 1996, 20.

"Readers' Forum on Black Male/Female Relationships." *Black Scholar*, May/June 1979, 14–67.

Saluter, Arlene F. "Singleness in America." U.S. Bureau of the Census, Current Population Reports Series P23, No. 175. *Population Trends in the 1980s*. Washington, DC: GPO, 1992.

Shockley, Ann Allen. *Say Jesus and Come to Me*. Tallahasee, FL: Naiad Press, Inc., 1987.

Singer, Barry. Liner notes for *Guess Who's in Town: Bobby Short Performs the Songs of Andy Razaf*. New York: Atlantic Recording Corporation, 1987.

Singleton, John. "Kiss of the Superwoman: Terry McMillan." *Esquire*, August 1995, 59.

Smith, Jessie Carrey, and Carrel P. Horton, eds. *Statistical Record of Black America*. Detroit: Gale Research, Inc., 1997.

Smitherman, Geneva. *Talking and Testifyin: The Language of Black America*. Detroit: Wayne State UP, 1986.

Stovall, TaRessa. "From Page to Screen." *Emerge*, March 1996, 38–42.

"Submission Guidelines." Genesis Press Web site, accessed August 25, 1998, at: *http://ebicom.net/genesis/submissions_guidelines.html*.

"Submission Guidelines for Arabesque Multi-Cultural Romance Line." Arabesque Web site, accessed August 25, 1998, at: *http://www. kensingtonbooks.com/arabesque.html*.

Taeuber, Cynthia. *Statistical Handbook on Women in America*. Phoenix, AZ: Oryx Press, 1991.

Tan, Amy. *The Joy Luck Club*. New York: G. P. Putnam's Sons, 1989.

Tate, Claudia. *Black Women Writers at Work*. New York: Continuum Publishing Company, 1993.

————. Introduction. *The Flagellants*, by Carlene Hatcher Polite. Boston: Beacon Press, 1987.

Terry, Wallace. *Bloods: An Oral History of the Vietnam War by Black Veterans*. New York: Ballantine Books, 1989.

"Terry's Children." *Essence*, February 1998, 74.

Trescott, Jacqueline. "The Urban Author: Straight to the Point." *Washington Post*, November 17, 1990.

Twain, Mark. *Adventures of Huckleberry Finn*. Ed. Gerald Graff and James Phelan. New York: Bedford Books, 1995.

U.S. Bureau of the Census. *Statistical Abstract of the U.S. 1978*. Washington, D.C.: U.S. Government Printing Office, 1978.

————. *Statistical Abstract of the U.S. 1988*. Washington, D.C.: U.S. Government Printing Office, 1988.

U.S. Department of Labor Office of Policy Planning and Research. *The Negro Family: The Case for National Action*. Washington, D.C.: U.S. Government Printing Office, 1965.

Wallace, Michele. *Black Macho and the Myth of the Super Woman*. New York: Dial Press, 1979.

Wideman, John Edgar. "Frame and Dialect: The Evolution of the Black Voice in American Literature." *American Poetry Review* 5, no. 5 (September/October 1976): 34–37.

Williams, Sherley Anne. "The Blues Roots of Contemporary African-American Poetry." In *Afro-American Literature: The Reconstruction of Instruction*, ed. Dexter Fisher and Robert B. Stepto. New York: Modern Language Association, 1979.

Wolcott, James. "Showcase: Terry McMillan." *New Yorker*, April 29, 1996, 102+

Woods, Paula L. "Isn't It Romantic." *Essence*, July 1997, 75.

Index

About the Author

PAULETTE RICHARDS is Assistant Professor of English at Loyola University in New Orleans where she teaches African-American literature and Creative Writing. She has published translations in *Callaloo* and presented papers on African American Science Fiction at National Popular Culture Association conferences.

Critical Companions to Popular Contemporary Writers

First Series—*also available on CD-ROM*

V. C. Andrews
by E. D. Huntley

Tom Clancy
by Helen S. Garson

Mary Higgins Clark
by Linda C. Pelzer

Arthur C. Clarke
by Robin Anne Reid

James Clavell
by Gina Macdonald

Pat Conroy
by Landon C. Burns

Robin Cook
by Lorena Laura Stookey

Michael Crichton
by Elizabeth A. Trembley

Howard Fast
by Andrew Macdonald

Ken Follett
by Richard C. Turner

John Grisham
by Mary Beth Pringle

James Herriot
by Michael J. Rossi

Tony Hillerman
by John M. Reilly

John Jakes
by Mary Ellen Jones

Stephen King
by Sharon A. Russell

Dean Koontz
by Joan G. Kotker

Robert Ludlum
by Gina Macdonald

Anne McCaffrey
by Robin Roberts

Colleen McCullough
by Mary Jean DeMarr

James A. Michener
by Marilyn S. Severson

Anne Rice
by Jennifer Smith

Tom Robbins
*by Catherine E. Hoyser and
Lorena Laura Stookey*

John Saul
by Paul Bail

Erich Segal
by Linda C. Pelzer

Gore Vidal
by Susan Baker and Curtis S. Gibson